The

RETIREMENT
SOLUTION

The
RETIREMENT
SOLUTION

*Cutting through the
Financial Lies, Junk,
and Misinformation*

JON HICKS

Printed in the United States of America.
Library of Congress Control Number: 2020905632
ISBN: 978-1-73425-832-5
Cover and Layout Design: Mary Hamilton

CONTENTS

Turn Off the News

L ife's a gas, and you want to enjoy it. Hell, you deserve to enjoy it. It's not like you'll get a second shot.

And maybe so far you've been enjoying life just fine. Maybe you've been successful. Maybe you've been *very* successful. Maybe you've been climbing-Kilimanjaro, spending-nights-in-Bali, surfing-in-Maui, bar-hopping-in-New-Orleans, walking-the-Great-Wall-of-China, sipping-Cristal-with-supermodels-at-the-Super-Bowl successful.

If that's you, *woo-hoo!* Like I said, life's a gas.

But ease off that pedal just a bit. I've got some questions I'd like to ask you.

Have you really thought this whole life deal through? Have you considered the possibility that you—yes, *you!*—might be eighty years old someday? Or ninety? Or one hundred?

Have you considered that if you're living too large today, you might find yourself living very small—and hating every minute of your diminished existence—someday in the future? And have you considered that your faraway future really isn't far away at all?

Trust me on this: your future will be upon you before you know it.

And here's the bottom line that you don't want to learn when it's too late: life's a gas—until you run out of gas.

* * *

So if you're a baby boomer or a Gen Xer or a millennial… I'm about to give you the best financial advice you'll ever get from anyone.

Turn off the TV.

That's it. Four words.

If it didn't quite sink in, I'll say it in all caps so you can hear it better.

TURN OFF THE TV! Do it now!

Turn it off because if you've been getting your financial advice from the talking heads on TV—if your money guru is Suze Orman or Jim Cramer or Stuart Varney or Dave Ramsey or Ric Edelman or any one of a few dozen others who are making a fortune telling you how to invest your hard-earned cash—then there's a good chance you're not going to be where you really want to be when you hit the end zone.

That's because the talking heads are feeding you junk.

That's right… junk.

They're all selling something, and they're *really* good at it. First and foremost, they're entertainers. They have to be because if they don't entertain, people won't watch. And if people don't watch, advertisers won't buy commercial time. And if advertisers don't buy commercial time, the TV networks won't want to keep paying the talking heads. They'll cancel the show and find someone else to sell you stuff.

The talking heads really have just one goal: to get new viewers and keep the ones they already have. They're not there for you; they're there for themselves. And they'll wave their arms and scream and yell and be as sensational as they can because that's what entertainers do if they want to keep you coming back for more.

They know you want to believe that what you hear is the truth. And they know you're primed to make some very poor choices based on what you hear.

P. T. Barnum knew what he was talking about: there's a sucker born every minute.

So don't be a sucker. Turn off the damn TV now!

* * *

OK... is it off? Can we talk?

I want to tell you what the talking heads don't want you to know: the truth. And no matter what Jack Nicholson said, I think you *can* handle the truth.

So here it is: no one knows what's going to happen in the financial future.

Everywhere you turn, someone with a great smile and lots of personality is telling you, or more likely shouting at you, that he— and he alone—has the crystal ball that reveals the future.

But the cold hard truth is he doesn't have a clue. I'll say it again: no one knows what's going to happen in the financial future.

The financial planning sector in America has become a haven for self-appointed experts and do-it-yourselfers. The financial networks, the financial print media, and a billion or so financial websites are basically selling us on the false concept that they, and they alone, know what's going to happen—and that they possess foolproof strategies for preventing financial loss.

Well, stop the presses. They don't.

I know this for a fact because I'm on TV and radio every week too. And what I've learned is that we are drowning in a sea of information. We're searching for wisdom from Google, but we have no idea whether what we're reading and hearing is even factual. And even if the "wisdom" you find on Google actually *is* factual, is that wisdom wise for *you*? For your spouse? For your kids?

What if the guy knows what he's talking about but he's not talking about *you*?

Back in the Stone Age, when I was growing up, there were only three TV stations and, of course, no internet. So the most I could get were three opinions.

> We're searching for wisdom from Google, but we have no idea whether what we're reading and hearing is even factual.

Now there are about eight hundred billion. The awful truth is that any idiot can go online, create a blog, and become an instant expert. That guy who says he's a forty-year-old billionaire could easily be an eight-year-old girl with three quarters and a dime in her piggy bank.

So do yourself a big favor right now. Make the best investment possible in your financial future: find a better source of information. And *turn off the damn TV!*

* * *

Here's what the talking heads on TV aren't telling you.

You need a real retirement solution, a plan for putting aside a portion of your income every time you get paid and for saving it intelligently so that the money you accumulate when you're working will be distributed back to you, on a regular, systematic schedule, when you choose to retire.

It's a real retirement solution that's tailored just for you, and it has nothing to do with products. It's very simple, really. You accumulate money when you can so that you can distribute it back to yourself when you can't. There's even a term for it: distribution economics, which we'll cover in great depth later. But you'll likely never hear that from the TV gurus.

It has to be a sensible plan. You don't want to retire early, start spending the money you've accumulated too soon, and find yourself broke and eating cat food at the age of eighty. You also don't want to die at the age of ninety-five as the richest person in the graveyard, wishing you'd had more fun when you were young and could have enjoyed it.

But it *is* possible. *You* can do this. It's not brain surgery—though it does require a brain.

But first, if it hasn't already, your brain should be telling you to turn off that mind-numbing TV. You've got work to do.

* * *

Things weren't always this way.

In the old days, a whole half century ago, you went to work, you earned a salary, and your employer offered you a pension plan that would send you a check every month for the rest of your life when you reached retirement age.

But pensions were *soooo* twentieth century. It wasn't broke, so we fixed it anyway.

We replaced pensions with 401(k)s and other investment vehicles that were designed to "put our future in our hands." The pitch was, and still is, that you should set aside a portion of your income and put it into a 401(k) plan. Then you can invest your money any way you want.

It all sounds great in theory, but it's truly a gamble. If you feel like putting all your money into Enron or Toys "R" Us, ain't nobody gonna stop you.

But hey, have a good time. Roll the dice. Maybe you'll roll a seven—or multiple sevens. And maybe you'll become so intoxicated with your success that you'll go all in. And then, sure enough, that's when you'll roll snake eyes.

You could be sitting pretty with lots of money stashed away for your retirement just to see the economy tank the day after you sail off into the sunset. And then suddenly you'll have to ditch that boat and go back to work—if you can still find it—because you no longer have even half the money you had one week before, when you quit.

Do you think it can't happen to you?

Well, it can. Ask those baby boomers who retired in 2007 and had to go back to work in 2009 because half their nest egg vanished in the Great Recession.

* * *

The only way to ensure a steady flow of dollars into your pockets after you retire is to set up the equivalent of a pension plan, one that's designed just for you and will perform regardless of what economic winds are blowing.

But you won't get that from the TV talking heads because what they're selling you has absolutely nothing to do with creating your retirement plan. It's 100 percent geared toward the products they sell.

They'll talk about an investment fund, and they'll tell you, "Look how great this fund company is! It beat the Lipper peer group average! It got a five-star Morningstar rating!"

Stop right there!

Ask yourself, What on earth is a Lipper peer group average? What the hell is a five-star Morningstar rating? Is that five out of five… or five out of fifty? I reckon it's better than four—I *hope* it's better than four—but really, what does it mean?

If you don't know, then why on earth do you care?

Because the talking heads say you should?

They're telling you these things because they're selling stuff. It's all a product pitch. They might as well be saying, "Less filling! Tastes great! Zero carbs! Gluten-free!"

At least you know what those things mean.

Lipper peer group averages and Morningstar ratings impress us because we fall in love with our favorite talking heads. If you're a Suze Orman fan and Suze says buy widgets because they have a five-star Morningstar rating, then you'll buy widgets. Maybe Jim Cramer says you should buy something else, but well, you know, he's not Suze. Why would you listen to Jim when you love Suze?

Because we're human, we gravitate toward the things we like. But it's easy to lose sight of our goals if we become too attached. If you follow Dave Ramsey, you may feel like you can follow him anywhere. But that's a huge mistake. This is your journey, not Dave's. He shouldn't be the one who decides which way you'll go when you hit a fork in the road.

The fact is Dave's never met you. He knows nothing about you. Neither do Suze, Cramer, Stuart, and Ric. They're giving you advice that's right for them, not for you. But the more you hear it, the more you think it has to be right.

Try to remember the first time you heard Taylor Swift. Maybe you liked her, maybe you didn't. But the more you heard her, the more her music got in your head. And the next thing you knew, you decided that she must be really good because her songs were being played on every radio station every minute of the day. Her latest hit got stuck in your head because you heard it constantly.

And that's all it took. Suddenly, you loved Taylor Swift.

That's what the talking heads do to you.

Financial advisors do it too. Sit down with them and they'll quickly throw a familiar name at you—Vanguard, American Funds, something you've heard of. They know that the name itself will command your respect and that you'll sign up for the plan when you hear it.

They know you like to hear something familiar, and they'll make you feel very comfortable when they tell you something you already know.

They had you before you even walked in the door.

But did you stop to consider that they get a little slice of every dollar you put into whatever instrument they recommend? Did you even consider that they might recommend an investment that puts a little more money in their pocket than a different one that might work better for you?

It's the same thing with the big financial companies. They want you for a client, but the truth is that they have a much more important client than you'll ever be—their shareholders.

Remember this: when you're sitting in front of a big financial company's broker, you're not alone. Though you can't see them, the company shareholders are sitting there right next to you. The broker can see them, and he cares a lot more about keeping them happy than he does you because they're the ones who pay his bills.

* * *

The modern financial model is built on a very simple premise: Save. Save. Save. Repeat. Build yourself a big old pile of money, and you'll be fine.

But that's only half the equation. The other half is now that you have yourself a big old pile of money, what are you going to do with it?

The fact is the way we grow money is different from the way we need to spend it. We're laser-focused on accumulation, and nobody wants to talk about distribution.

Nobody asks the big question: now that I've got this big old pile of money, how can I effectively live on that for twenty, thirty, or forty years?

I've talked about this with more baby boomers than I can count, and so many of them have told me the same thing. Their top fear—their absolute number one—is that they'll run out of money.

They tell me, "Well, I have these products that I've always heard of and everyone says are great. So how come I'm still afraid I'll run out of money?"

Here's how come: because they don't have a real strategy. They've been taught to invest their money for the sake of investment, and nobody's ever told them how to make sure it won't run out.

They don't have a legitimate game plan. They don't know where they are, and they're being led astray by financial marketers.

What they need is a budget they can stick to and understand, one that will leave them feeling that even if the worst happens, they'll be OK.

It won't be fancy. But if they stick to it, it'll work.

And it'll work for you too.

The first thing you need to know is that saving for retirement isn't one size fits all. There are too many variables: When do you want to retire? How much income do you need? Do you have a spouse? Kids? Do you want to leave a legacy, or could you care less? Do you want to finance your grandkids' college educations, or do you want your very last check—the one that goes to your undertaker—to bounce?

This is your call. You're not your neighbor. What's right for her may be all wrong for you. The key is to know exactly where you are at all times, but that's easier said than done.

* * *

When I was a kid, my parents used to pile my brother and me into the family car and head down to Hilton Head each year. We belonged to AAA—this was before dashboard navigation systems and smartphones—and they had this thing called a TripTik, a booklet of maps on which an agent marked your route in bright green marker to show you where you were going and what you'd find along the way.

But the one thing that TripTik couldn't show you was where you were at any given moment. You could see where you came from, and you could see where you were going, but you kept finding yourself saying, "Where are we now?"

That perfectly describes the state of our finances today. You know where you want to go, but you don't know which way to turn—or when—because you don't really know where you are.

You say, "Oh well, I'm in Vanguard. I hear that's great. I must be fine."

Are you?

Maybe you hear that annuities are good, so you'll invest in annuities, and then there'll be nothing to worry about. You'll be fine.

Will you?

The fact is you have no way of knowing because you haven't established where you are. How can you possibly know which way to go?

Robert Frost took the road less traveled, but he had only two choices. Who knows what he might have done if he had come to a five-way crossing?

Here's the bottom line: you need to know exactly where you are so you can eliminate all the paths in front of you that won't take you where you want to go.

And you won't get there by comparing your path to someone else's. Whatever you do, *don't compare*! Just because something works for your buddy or your neighbor doesn't mean it's going to work for you. Teddy Roosevelt said, "Comparison is the thief of joy," and he knew what he was talking about.

Maybe you've been writing for years with an old Bic pen with a blue plastic cap that you've pretty much chewed through, and then you discover that the guy in the next cubicle has this fancy new gel pen. It's awesome. It has a textured rubber grip, and it's so smooth. You just have to have one.

So you buy one, and the next thing you know you've got ink all over your shirt.

That's what happens when you compare. And I get it because I do it too.

Let me tell you about my air fryer... yep, those late-night TV gadgets that make you hungry and excited at the same time... Well, I had a perfectly good one, but then one of my friends started raving about this new one he'd just bought. It was a beauty, with lots of buttons and LEDs and a few dozen settings, and he said it was awesome and I just had to get one.

It looked really nice, and I had a 20-percent-off coupon from Bed Bath & Beyond burning a hole in my pocket, so I bought the thing.

And you know what? It wasn't as good as the one I already had. I trusted an unreliable opinion, and I got suckered by the marketers.

I was an idiot. I compared.

We do that with pens and air fryers and refrigerators and cars. We do it with our finances, too, and Wall Street takes advantage of that. If you get it in your head that your neighbor's investment plan is better than yours, the financial giants will be happy to help you switch—even if it's the wrong thing for you. They're in the business of keeping the customer satisfied. And you're a customer.

So don't compare. Your best friend's investment plan may be right for him, but it may be all wrong for you.

* * *

The largest brokerage companies love to create TV commercials showing people in their sixties, with their perfect teeth, toned bodies, and silver hair, driving along the coastline with the top down in a classic convertible, the sun in their face and the wind in their hair.

That's their pitch, and it's seductive as hell. They want to put that image in your head and make you think you can have it all—if you buy their product.

But come on—do you think they know what road *you're* on, or what road you really want to be on? What if you're not big on oceanside drives? What if you'd rather be driving a Winnebago in Minnesota?

What if what they're selling is all wrong for you?

The truth is they're selling accumulation. Keep putting your money into their accounts, and you'll be driving that convertible someday. It's sexy, and sex sells.

Distribution, on the other hand, isn't sexy. But it's where the math points, and you need to understand it if you're going to have a real retirement solution. Here's why.

Let's say you've managed to save a million bucks for retirement, and you're thinking, "A million bucks! Woohoo!"

Now let's take a serious look at what that really means. Let's face the unappealing fact that because interest rates are low, you can probably pull out only about 2.8 percent of your million bucks every year if you want it to last for twenty or thirty years.[1]

Do you know what 2.8 percent of a million bucks is? It's $28,000. That's how much you can take out of your million bucks every year if you want it to last: $28,000.

What? Hold on there! How can I have $1 million in the bank and end up being able to take out only $28,000 a year? *How can that possibly be?*

It's because it's math, and math doesn't lie. It may reveal some unappealing truths, but you can't dispute it.

That's the distribution side of the real retirement solution. It isn't sexy, but if you don't plan for it—and if you forget to die young—you'll regret it.

See the video that discusses withdrawal rates at
www.StormproofRetirement.com

---

1   According to a recent study by David Blanchett, head of retirement research in the investment management division at Morningstar Inc., 2.8 percent is the maximum withdrawal rate from retirement portfolios over a thirty-year period.

* * *

My granddad had federal and state pensions. He never made more than $32,000 a year while he was working, but his pensions were paying him $111,000 every year by the time he died. He had savings, but he didn't really need them. His pension plan paid him nearly ten grand a month, every month, no matter what.

That was financial freedom.

It had nothing to do with how much he accumulated. The freedom was in the distribution: knowing that the money would be coming in, just as he had planned, every month without fail.

It was all about consistency, which is the key to a real retirement solution. It's what will leave you sleeping comfortably at night.

The Baseball Hall of Famer Ralph Kiner famously said, "Home run hitters drive Cadillacs. Singles hitters drive Fords."

Kiner hit a lot of home runs, and he drove Cadillacs, and he dated some gorgeous women. But sluggers tend to sizzle, then fizzle. He was in the major leagues for only ten years.

Home run hitters may be the most popular players—and, yes, they get to drive the Cadillac—but they generally don't stick around as long as the great singles hitters, the guys like Rod Carew and Ichiro Suzuki who get two hundred base hits year after year after year.

They drive the Ford, but they drive it for a long time.

That's what you want from your real retirement solution—consistency.

If you're driving a Caddy during your accumulation years, then good for you.

But never forget: there's a Ford in your future. Make sure you can afford it.

CHAPTER ONE

From Wall Street to Tim McGraw

I s the TV still off?

Good. Let's move on. It's time I gave you the second best piece of financial advice you'll ever get from anyone.

Right now, if you haven't already, you need to ask yourself the following question: *who is this guy?*

Seriously. Here I am telling you to turn off your television, to stop listening to talking heads with perfect hair and wide smiles, to close your browser and stop taking advice from mysterious, self-appointed gurus on the internet. I'm telling you to do things that are essentially heretical in our wired culture, so you really should be asking…

Who is this guy?

Good question. Glad you asked.

I grew up in a small farm town outside of Owensboro, Kentucky. My dad was a judge and small-town attorney, and my mother taught third grade at the local elementary school. Even though we didn't really know it as kids, we grew up "rural poor." Our small ranch house backed up to tobacco fields and cow pastures. Most of my father's clients were farmers who often paid their bills through barter. They would bring us tomatoes, fresh-baked pies, and homemade sausage or offer to bushhog some of our property to pay Dad. So my mom's teacher salary often had to pay the bills for a family of four.

It was in college that I realized that understanding finances was the way to do better for my family. We never discussed finances growing up—it was considered poor manners. But the families of my college friends who seemed to have all the money in the world talked about money. They seemed to understand it. So I focused on studying economics and finance. I went on to get a master of business administration and a master of financial services and then finished up with postgraduate financial management through Cornell University.

For the past twenty years, I've been in the wealth management industry, helping investors cut through the crap so they can be confident in their retirement plans.

I'm a fiduciary.

Stay with me here because that word—*fiduciary*—is really important. It means my clients pay me a flat fee for my financial advice. I get nothing—zero, nada, bupkis—from the investment vehicles I recommend for their securities portfolios. I receive no incentive fees or percentages whatsoever. I work for and get paid by my clients, and only my clients.

But I wasn't always a fiduciary. I started out on Wall Street.

I worked for a large brokerage firm and learned all the stuff I was supposed to: how to properly diversify a portfolio, how to beat the Lipper peer group average. All that nonsense.

I was pretty good at it too. I started in 1998–99, during the dot-com boom, when everything was humming. I looked for five-star funds that were doing great—and not ones that coincidentally paid me a handsome commission—and sat back with a big smile on my face as all my clients made tons of money.

I did all the things I was supposed to do… but I never really asked myself who was benefitting the most—my brokerage firm (and me) or my client? Even if I'd thought to ask, I had no real reason to. Everyone was doing great.

That is, they were doing great… until they weren't. The new millennium arrived, the bubble burst, and people lost half their life savings.

* * *

I specifically remember a client who said to me, "You know, Jon, I'm not a very rich woman. I never married. I've got $250,000, and I'm thinking about retiring in ten years. Do you think what you're telling me to do will work?"

I put on my magic broker hat and earnestly replied, "Well, Ms. Smith, if we go with a properly diversified portfolio of yadda yadda mutual blah blah blah funds and we get a nominal 7 percent yadda yadda blah blah blah return, you'll double your money in ten years, and you'll be able to live a very happy life."

I conveniently neglected to mention that the mutual funds I was recommending would pay me more than some others I might have suggested because *why should I?*

I was a broker, and that's what brokers are taught to do.

Fast-forward two years, and Miss Smith was no longer a client of mine. To this day, I suspect it had something to do with the fact that she'd lost half her money and that her prospects of retiring comfortably in ten years had vanished with it.

And that was when it dawned on me that the advice I was offering my clients was all about business—for me, not for them. For them, it was personal.

I had done everything I was supposed to do. I'd recommended the investment vehicles my company said I should, and I'd gotten paid handsomely for doing so. But I had to face the fact that my company-approved recommendations had done serious financial damage to a nice woman who trusted me.

Now, think about this for a minute: no broker is ever held liable for that. I gave lousy advice to a nice woman, and I suffered no repercussions whatsoever. Neither did any of my peers. Brokers say they know what's right for their clients, and their clients trust them because they believe they're looking out for them. But it just ain't so.

I did everything according to the book, and I made very good money. I was the apple of my employer's eye. But that was because I'd been looking out for my company and myself.

I should have been looking out for my clients, but I wasn't. None of us were.

I had blinders on. We *all* had blinders on. The brokerages that paid us wanted us to focus on one thing and one thing only: what lay straight ahead of us.

They didn't want us to look around to see if there were better options for our clients. Our clients were what made them money. Our clients were the sale.

The sale is what creates profits for shareholders—and the shareholders are much more important to the company than the clients. If you lose a client, that's OK. Go find another. Just keep the shareholders satisfied.

But now, after eight years of seeing only what was in front of me, my blinders were suddenly coming off, and I could see what was going on all around me.

There was no way I could put those blinders back on.

* * *

I remember my first day. They threw a phone book at me and said, "Here you go, kid. We're gonna tell you what to say on the phone. Now say it, and earn your keep."

I remember thinking, "Hell, I've got an MBA. This is crap. Why am I doing it?"

But that thought didn't last long. I was working in an occupation that was held in high esteem, just like an attorney or a physician—only, if I was good at it, I could make a lot more money than a physician.

But to be good at it, I had to sell, sell, sell.

So I sold, sold, sold—until I realized I wasn't really helping the people who were listening to me.

And once you realize that, you know you have to stop.

But stopping isn't as easy as it sounds because now you face a serious dilemma: Are you willing to make less money? How much? How about a *lot* less money? Even if you're willing, is your spouse? (How you gonna keep them down on the farm once they've seen Paris?) Is changing your career track a step in the right direction—or will it land you in divorce court?

Well, I was going to find out. Because having taken off the blinders, there was no way I could put them back on.

So I became a fiduciary, which meant I worked only for the client. It was a huge risk for me personally because I would no longer get paid by a brokerage and I'd stop receiving commissions and percentages of my clients' investments.

But it also meant that I no longer would be working for a company that told me what to tell my client. It meant that I no longer would be told, "You have to sell this. You have a quota."

Once I became a fiduciary, clients would pay me for my advice and for implementing a plan that was best for them, whether that meant buying investment property in Florida, cattle in Texas, movie theaters in California, Broadway shows in New York, or a safe and sound mutual fund.

Whatever my advice, it would be what I thought was best for my client, not for a brokerage.

And it was only then, when I was gone, that my eyes opened wide. I found out that my brokerage firm got compensated 4 or 5 percent a year out of my client's money. And that was mind numbing because I hadn't been aware of it. Of course, it was in my best interest as a salesman not to know because knowing would have made me feel lousy, and then I would have been a terrible employee, and then I would have been fired. If I kept my blinders on, I'd be driving a Lexus and trading it in for a new one every year. If I became a fiduciary, I'd be trading that Lexus in for a used Kia.

But I didn't want to be a salesman. I don't think anyone who becomes a broker does. It doesn't say *salesman* on the business card. It says *Financial Advisor*. But really, it should just say salesman because that's what being a broker is all about: hardcore sales.

* * *

As it turned out, people started to pay attention. People would ask me, "Why do you sound so different from the guy I'm working with now? How come I can see mathematically what you're saying?"

They'd tell me, "This actually makes sense. I was going on my guy's best judgment, and it didn't blow up, so I assumed it was true. But what you're saying corresponds to how I feel, and you're proving it mathematically. Why are you so different?"

And I'd say, "Well, fiduciaries and brokers are not really the same animal. They're in the same family, but they're very different. It's like comparing a wolf to a guide dog. I'm not here to eat you up; I'm here to keep you on your feet."

And I guess the word got around because the next thing I knew, my local radio station invited me on to do a segment on how to save for retirement.

I didn't know what I was doing—I had no experience or training for this—but what I said on air must have resonated with the audience because the station then asked if I'd like to do a regular show.

The only thing I knew was that I had a face for radio. But I thought about it for a while, and I decided that talking into a mic would give me a real opportunity to make my point. I could say, "Hey, listen... you're probably not in a bad spot, and you probably are with someone very good and reputable, and maybe you've been with them for a long time.

"But hear me out. You might want to consider exploring your options and finding out whether what you're doing actually makes mathematical sense and is right for you.

"Not for your next-door neighbor. Not for your brother. Not for your colleague...

"You."

People had never heard that before. They'd never heard someone say, "Hey, I don't care what you do, but at the very least I'd like you to take a minute to figure out whether what you're doing is best for you. And by the way, you're more than welcome to take my advice back to your guy. See what he says. Chances are he's not gonna like it because he's gonna get paid a lot less money. But really, shouldn't this be up to you, not him?"

* * *

That message started to resonate—and then it took on a soundtrack.

I worked with a consulting firm that wanted to get more people to tune in to the show, and it hatched a plan that was nothing short of brilliant.

Entertainers were always coming into town to play at the KFC Yum! Center or some other local venue in Louisville, and they wanted to promote their concerts and their albums. So they'd come to the studio to drum up business.

In New York, they go on *Colbert* or *Fallon*. In Los Angeles, they go on *Kimmel* or *Ellen*. In Louisville, Kentucky, it was Jon Hicks on *The Retirement Solution*, 840 WHAS on your AM dial, every Sunday morning right after church.

We'd bring in performers who were at retirement age or who would be soon. They'd provide us with CDs to give away, and we'd get to ask them some questions about what they planned to do in the years to come:

When—if—you ever stop performing… what next?

Are you ever gonna retire?

Do you feel like you have enough? Is enough ever really enough?

If you could do anything that you wanted to do right now, what would you do?

We brought on some big-name stars—Brad Paisley, Tim McGraw, Sammy Hagar, Chicago, the Doobie Brothers—and you know what we found out?

They're just like the rest of us.

They want to do what they like.

No matter how much money they have, they're probably not going to retire because they're having too good a time doing what they're doing.

And there you have it. That's the key.

Retirement isn't a date. It isn't the day you turn sixty-five or seventy or seventy-five, a magic moment in time when you just call it quits and settle into a rocking chair.

If you're doing what you love, why would you ever stop doing it—especially if you can get paid? It's not like these guys need the money, though there are some who do. It's more like they're still getting paid to do what they love, so why would they want to stop?

Some said they keep performing because they want to stay relevant, which I've found to be a typical male response. They don't necessarily have a huge network of friends outside of their work, and they have a hard time finding what they consider to be a meaningful and relevant place in society when they hang it up.

Most guys, I've found, don't want to go babysit the grandkids every day. Some do, but it seems to be mostly the grandmothers who want that. The guys tend to feel that changing diapers, wiping runny noses, and putting Band-Aids on scrapes isn't what they were put on this planet to do. They want to stay relevant.

One of our most intriguing guests was Sammy Hagar. He came on the show and basically said, "After I got kicked out of Van Halen, I found myself asking what I was gonna do with my time. I did a couple things after that with some pretty cool bands, but what I really wanted to do was just perform and drink."

OK, fair enough. He's entitled. And the great thing is… he pulled it off! He went to Cabo San Lucas, Mexico; bought a tequila factory; and opened up a nightclub called Cabo Wabo. He ended up selling the factory for more money than he ever made with Van Halen, but he kept Cabo Wabo. And what does he do now? He plays there three, four, maybe six nights a week, whatever feels right. And he loves it.

Sammy didn't know that was his retirement dream. He wouldn't even call it retirement. It's just living. Why should he even think of quitting?

There were others, though, who felt they had to keep on working because they never knew when their stars might fade.

One of those was Peter Frampton. Back in the seventies, he became a superstar. His light shone very bright, but it quickly dimmed. When we brought him on to our show, he was working because he needed to. He said he'd never realized that fame can be fleeting, and he hadn't planned for what might come when his albums stopped going platinum.

* * *

Our show clicked. After a while, the producers said we didn't sound like anyone else out there, so why not speak into a larger megaphone?

And the next thing we knew, we were hosting a TV show. This made-for-radio face was suddenly wearing makeup on television. But we still have the radio show too.

* * *

What I've learned from our shows is this: we're all in the same boat.

Some of the celebrities who appear on our show are working for love. Others are working because they need to or because they're trying to maintain their relevance or their lifestyle.

People think they all have mansions, and they're all paid for— but that's just not true. Mötley Crüe had many cars repossessed over the years. 50 Cent was worth tens of millions of dollars at one point, and he still went broke. Sammy Hagar, frankly, lucked out when he bought that tequila factory.

And then there are those who decided that the best way to stay relevant was to reinvent themselves entirely. One of our guests who did that was Darius Rucker, who was known for years as the front man of the nineties pop group Hootie and the Blowfish. The group did great for five years or so, but they ultimately faded from the charts. When that happened, Rucker didn't just fold up his tent. He went home to South Carolina and recreated himself as a country music star.

He didn't quit; he reinvented himself, and now he loves what he's doing.

Just don't call him Hootie. He doesn't like that.

* * *

What happened to Darius Rucker and Sammy Hagar is the sort of thing that can happen to anyone, whether they're let go or downsized or maybe even when they discover that they just hate their job. It doesn't happen only to celebrities—it can happen to you too. But if you save well (and it doesn't have to be a lot) and you have the right plan, you can recover. Do things right, and when the time comes to stop doing what you've been doing throughout your career, you'll be able to do something bold and different.

Maybe you won't do it for love or for a passion, but if you prepare correctly, you'll know where you are and where you want to go when the time comes to go there.

All you need is a dream and a plan to make it come true. Life has a funny way of putting us in our place. But never—*never*—forget how to dream.

> # Life has a funny way of putting us in our place. But never—never—forget how to dream.

So ask yourself, What do you want to do with the rest of your life? Do you want to go back to your roots? Do you want to branch out in a whole new direction? How do you want to stay relevant?

These are critical questions, and you should never stop asking them. You want to prepare so you'll be able to act on your answers.

Your chance will come. That day will be yours. Make sure you can seize it.

Tony Robbins, the motivational speaker, talks about this all the time. I've heard him say that when he talked to Carly Simon, she told him she felt fear every time she stepped on a stage. She said her heart would start racing, she would start getting nervous, and she would get horrible pains in her stomach.

And then Robbins spoke with Bruce Springsteen, who told him that he *loved* going out there on the stage. His heart would start racing, he'd get this feeling of excitement in his stomach, and he'd know he was ready.

Same situation. Same symptoms. Two people with the exact same feelings and polar opposite reactions to them.

That's how it is in retirement. What's right for the other guy won't necessarily be right for you. Money comes, and money goes, but your retirement years can be what you want them to be—if you plan correctly.

You'll need to understand distribution economics. And you'll need a real retirement plan that will provide you with a steady, guaranteed income when you quit working. Really, we need three to four income streams in retirement to ensure we will be taken care of.

And that plan will have to be a solid one, strong enough to weather any storm. Even a perfect storm.

Because I promise you, a perfect storm is coming.

See the video of the Perfect Storm at
www.StormproofRetirement.com/news

The Perfect Storm

I'm writing this book in the middle of the Atlantic hurricane season, so let's pause for a few minutes and talk about the weather. We all know what extreme weather can do.

Extended, severe heat waves can devastate crops, overload the electric grid, and—at their worst—kill hundreds or even thousands of elderly and ill people. Severe cold snaps can be similarly deadly for people who are homeless or do not have adequate heating in their homes. Severe thunderstorms can spawn tornadoes, electric storms can spark wildfires, and heavy rainstorms can cause flash flooding.

Cyclones, typhoons, and hurricanes—massive storms that start out as mere tropical depressions over ocean waters—can destroy everything in their path. A Category 3 hurricane can tear the roof off your house; a Category 4 or 5 hurricane can pulverize it. A hurricane of any category, in the wrong place and at the wrong time, can result in unbearable loss of life.

And then there are perfect storms, collisions of weather systems that create behemoths that are greater than the sum of their parts—storms that can leave unexpected, unpredictable, and often unimaginable damage in their wake.

A perfect storm occurred along the East Coast in late October of 2012, when Tropical Storm Sandy, which had never been stronger than a Category 1 hurricane in the Atlantic, made landfall just south of New York City.

It turned out Sandy was no ordinary tropical storm because she didn't barrel in alone. As she was moving north off the East Coast, an unusual dip in the jet stream pushed her west, and she collided with a winter-like storm system that was moving eastward over land. The storms merged to become a new storm system: a one-thousand-mile-wide perfect storm that became known as Superstorm Sandy.

Aided by a full moon that raised the tide level, Sandy pounded the shoreline with high winds and record-breaking storm surges. In higher elevations to the west, the conditions were blizzard-like.

By the time the skies had cleared, Sandy had devastated the New York and New Jersey coastline, turning streets into beaches, sparking an electric fire that burned down a neighborhood, uprooting board-walks like Tinkertoys, and leaving a New Jersey amusement park sitting in the ocean. She poured ocean water into New York City, flooding tunnels between boroughs and cutting power to nearly half of Manhattan. Her storm surge pushed back the waters of the Hudson River and flooded towns and power plants in the counties to the north. In some large and heavily populated areas, it took weeks—even months—to restore power.

More than seven years later, the New York metropolitan area is still coping with the aftermath. Along an entire subway line, service remains crippled while workers replace electrical switches in a tunnel under the East River. Those switches were damaged beyond repair by the salt water from the storm.

Superstorm Sandy has company in recent US history. Another perfect storm occurred in 1991, also in late October, when the remnants of Hurricane Grace merged with a nor'easter over the Canadian Maritimes and then reconstituted itself into a new, unnamed hurricane off New England.

That hurricane never made landfall, but it produced coastal flooding from New Jersey to New England. In the Atlantic, it created forty- to eighty-foot waves, one of which is thought to have capsized and destroyed the *Andrea Gail*, a fishing boat out of Massachusetts that had eight crewmen aboard.

Why do I say, "thought to have capsized"? Because after a search that covered 186,000 nautical square miles, no bodies were ever recovered. All that was found from the boat were an emergency radio beacon, fuel drums, a fuel tank, and an empty life raft.

That perfect storm and the loss of the *Andrea Gail* was recounted in Sebastian Junger's 1997 book, *The Perfect Storm*, and again three years later in Wolfgang Petersen's movie based on the book. The movie, like the book, was a best seller. How could it not be? It starred Mark Wahlberg and George Clooney.

* * *

By now you're probably thinking, "I thought this was a book about creating a real retirement solution. Why the hell is this guy talking about storms and ships and tossing around names like Sandy and Grace and Gail and Mark and George?"

Glad you asked. Here's why.

If you're looking for a perfect analogy for the financial landscape we're all facing today, you'd be hard pressed to find a better one than a perfect storm.

Maybe you've got a nice retirement plan that's designed to withstand inflation… or deflation… or a recession. But can your plan sustain multiple hits—a perfect storm of financial events—all at once?

It had better because a perfect financial storm, like a perfect weather storm, is not a single storm. It's a convergence of multiple storms. Right now five separate financial storms are forming in our nation's capital, and I promise you that they are edging closer to a head-on collision:

- Our country is flat broke, which means taxes will—not *may*—have to go up.

- We've bought too much crap on credit, and we'll soon be getting a call from the debt collector. It's time to pay up.

- Wall Street is selling us junk. It's taking our money, wrapping it up, and selling it to the next guy.

- We've lost our pensions, which used to be our security blankets. Without them, we're standing naked in the cold.

- We are emotionally wired to lose money. Time and again, we are doomed to see our feelings betray us.

Those are the five financial storms that are coming together to form a perfect storm—and you're exposed.

So put on your life vest. You're gonna need it.

* * *

The storyline of *The Perfect Storm* parallels our current financial climate perfectly.

Clooney's character, Billy Tyne, the captain of the *Andrea Gail*, was pretty much broke in the fall of 1991. Desperate to bring in some money as the end of the fishing season approached, he decided to go out on a final, late-season run. He gathered a small, hodge-podge crew that had never worked together, and they headed out to sea from Gloucester, Massachusetts.

And what, you say, does that have to do with your retirement solution?

Glad you asked. Let me explain.

Getting ready to retire is like being on the shore, making your plans, assembling your crew, preparing the boat, and finding someone to captain it.

When you retire, you'll be on that boat, out at sea, basically at the mercy of the captain and the elements. So you need to be mindful while you're still ashore of the fact that you can't control the elements—but you *can* control your captain. You need to find someone who knows the waters you'll be navigating, someone who has already confronted the elements that await you and has the skills and knowledge to navigate your boat safely through them.

While you're still on shore—while you're still working and making money—it's natural to think in stormy weather, "I'll be OK... Everything will be all right... I'm working. I'm doing what I have to do."

> But when you get on that retirement boat and head out to sea, the choice to keep on working will be gone.

But when you get on that retirement boat and head out to sea, the choice to keep on working will be gone. You'll have to buy into whatever is going on—good or bad, up or down, left or right—and you'll have to depend on your captain to steer you through.

It's either that or jump off the boat. And if you do the latter, you'd better be one helluva swimmer because you'll be abandoning ship in the eye of the storm.

In other words, you'll really have no choice at all. You'll have already made your choices, and at that point you'll have to live with them. You'll have to trust that your captain knows what he's doing and will pull you through—because he'll be all you've got.

* * *

This brings us back to Captain Clooney. The way he put his crew together was not very different from how we put together our own team of financial advisors when we contemplate retirement. We go out and find a tax guy, an insurance guy, and a finance guy. But more often than not, we find them all separately.

Maybe they've worked together before. Or maybe not. Maybe they don't even know each other.

And maybe you don't know them either. Maybe you don't really know anything about them at all.

Consider this: The crew of the *Andrea Gail* knew for sure that their captain had experience. But they didn't know he was desperate for money. Do you think this can't happen in the financial industry? How do you know if the broker you've found is giving you true, unbiased advice? How do you know he isn't selling you something because he needs to make a mortgage payment or put his kids through college?

You don't know. For all you know, his brokerage firm could be having trouble, and he needs to produce some profits *now*.

For all you know, you've chosen a captain whose ship is sinking. Now consider this too.

Once the *Andrea Gail* was out at sea, things didn't work out the way Captain Clooney planned. The fish weren't biting where they dropped their lines, so they headed out even farther, hoping their luck would change.

And, lo and behold, it did. They found a spot that was loaded with fish, and they caught more than they needed or wanted, more than they could have ever imagined. But when they did, they were so far out to sea that the ice they'd brought with them was melting, and the fish were rotting.

They had a boat filled with fish, but it would spoil before they returned to land.

They'd achieved awesome accumulation, but they were going to have terrible distribution.

The same thing happens to a lot of people who accumulate large retirement nest eggs—401(k)s and IRAs that look great on paper—but don't consider what will happen when they start to draw funds from them. They save and they save, but they're unaware that they're accumulating wealth all wrong because taxes, inflation, and market losses can ruin the catch. It's only when they retire that they discover they weren't really prepared. They have failed to foresee a foreseeable storm, and now that it's arrived, it's going to cripple them.

* * *

There's a moral to this story: understand the choices you make.

Captain Clooney chose poorly. He had a gazillion choices, and he made the wrong ones. Maybe he asked the wrong people for advice. Or maybe he cobbled together a crew of capable men who just didn't work well together. Whatever the reason, he found himself out in the Atlantic, too far from land, with a big pile of rotting fish and multiple storms converging on him.

He was doomed, just like so many of today's "savvy" investors with their wonderful 401(k)s. They're out there trying to captain their ships, but far too many of them don't realize that they're in over their heads.

The problem is that they *feel* that they're good. Maybe they survive a few rainstorms and high winds, and they think they're great. But then, at exactly the wrong time, when their guard is down, a perfect storm arrives. And now they're stuck in the middle of the ocean without a life raft that they can jump into when their boat breaks apart.

They're going to drown.

Today, as I'm writing this, the financial waters are relatively calm. But it's hurricane season, and I promise you the waters won't stay calm forever. The sea will become choppy. The wind will pick up. It will start to rain. Maybe it'll be a short storm, and you'll come out OK. But maybe it won't be. Maybe the sea will be rough, and the wind will howl, and the rain will come down in sheets. If that happens, maybe you won't survive.

> Today, as I'm writing this, the financial waters are relatively calm. But it's hurricane season, and I promise you the waters won't stay calm forever.

Here's the bottom line: if you don't want to go down with your sinking ship, you need to prepare to ride out a perfect storm.

The good news is... you can.

* * *

You know why Boy Scouts learn how to tie knots? No, it's not for the hell of it. It's because someday those kids might actually need to know how to tie knots. It goes hand in hand with the Boy Scouts' motto: be prepared.

Try to keep that motto in mind when you're devising a financial strategy for your retirement. You can't have a strategy for coping with something that you refuse even to acknowledge may happen.

So acknowledge it. Be prepared.

Here's a very basic fact: far too many people planning their retirement solutions don't understand what's going on financially, and they don't see the risks they're taking. They're getting bad advice and making bad decisions because they don't see the storms gathering strength on the horizon.

They see an economy that's been booming for almost a decade, and they base their retirement solutions on the ridiculous notion that it will continue to do so. They're thinking what goes up won't come down.

But what if what goes up *does* come down? What if the economy stumbles? What if it plummets? What if it does a perfect dive off the high board and face plants into an empty pool?

Here's a good strategy for planning your retirement: look before you leap. Know what's waiting for you down there at the bottom.

Today's retirement investment plans—the IRAs and 401(k) s that replaced old-fashioned pension plans—give us the power to captain our own ship. Today, every one of us can thump our chest and proclaim, "It's *my* retirement, it's *my* retirement plan, and I'm perfectly qualified and able to decide what's best for me."

Is that you? If it is, please… think about the last book you read on distribution economics or the negative amortization of stock prices. Show me your MBA from Wharton. Prove to yourself that you understand the realities of market loss. Please tell me you've studied what Nobel Prize winners have to say about active distribution and the consistency of income streams.

If you can do all that... great! But if you can't—or if you're not really sure you can—then maybe it's time to stop listening to the financial marketers who say you're the only one you need.

Because they're lying to you.

They're offering you crap, and they want you to buy it. You don't know them, and they don't know you. What makes you think they have your best interests in mind?

Consider for a moment the misinformation they feed us every day.

"Oh, the market's soaring," they say. "Just stay in it, and watch your money grow."

"Taxes? Don't worry about taxes. You're going to be in a lower tax bracket in retirement."

"Don't worry; nothing can go wrong in the long term. And even if something does, the government will take care of you if you run out of money. You'll have Social Security... Medicare... Medicaid."

Oh yeah? Do you really believe that?

The first thing you have to keep in mind is that nothing is assured. There are no guarantees. The government created these benefits, and the government can take them away—especially if it has no money to pay for them.

Or maybe the government *won't* take them away. Keeping them will be a piece of cake—if it dramatically raises taxes to cover the shortfall.

And if the government does that, how do you think you're gonna feel when you start withdrawing your tax-deferred income and your tax rate is suddenly and unexpectedly 10 or 20 or 30 percent higher than it was when you decided to defer paying it?

I'll tell you how you'll feel. You'll feel like you screwed up. And in case you forget, your spouse will be there to remind you.

So please… don't be that person. Don't fall into the trap of telling yourself, "Hey, well, everything's been fine for a while. The market keeps going up. Tax rates are going down. I made a whole bunch of money last year, I've got the wind at my back, and this ship is steering itself. Let's just stay on course."

Listen, bud, the wind is gonna change. Bet on it.

* * *

In the chapters that follow, we're going to talk about the things that are staring us straight in the face—the five storms that are taking shape and getting ready to converge, creating a perfect storm that will affect all of us: tax problems, lack of savings, market misinformation, the theft of our pensions, and our own emotions.

Will this perfect storm really come together? I can't tell you with absolute certainty that it will. But I can tell you that the forecast is ominous. There's a storm a-comin', and it looks like it'll be a big one.

So grab your raincoat. Don't be Captain Clooney.

Be prepared.

See the video on preparation at
www.StormproofRetirement.com/prepare

CHAPTER THREE

Storm No. 1

Our Government Is Flat Broke

sk anyone who's ever fled an approaching storm or hunkered down to ride one out, and they'll tell you it's not something you want to do quickly. You're in the crosshairs, so you'd better be ready. Develop a plan. Be prepared.

If you decide to flee, that means checking the tires, filling up the tank, getting cash out of an ATM, gathering your family members, your pets, and your precious possessions… and having a destination in mind—somewhere you can stay until it's safe to go home.

If you decide to ride it out, it means installing hurricane shutters or taping or boarding up your windows… sandbagging your home's perimeter… filling the tub… stocking your shelves with nonperishable foods, batteries, and bottled water.

Or you can go with door number three: stick your head in the sand, ignore the rising surf and the blowing winds and the clouds forming on the horizon, cross your fingers, and pray that sucker does a one-eighty and heads back out to sea.

The head-in-the-sand option is the easiest—and it's what we've been doing for far too long in the face of the first big storm that's heading our way.

Let's call it Hurricane Destitution. Brother, can you spare 235 trillion dimes?

* * *

The fact is our country is broke. Tapped out. We're living on borrowed money, and well, you know how the song goes… Nobody loves you when you're down and out.

Listen closely. Do you hear the phone ringing? It's the collection bureau.

Now, what are you gonna do about it?

Here's an idea: tonight, after dinner, gather your kids and grandkids by the fireplace. Tell them to put their precious smartphones down for a minute and pay attention for a change. Then look them straight in the eye and say, "Kids, I want to share with you an important decision I've made…

"I have decided to ruin your future."

That's right. You tell them that—because it's the truth. You broke the piggy bank.

But… but… what's that you say? We're the greatest country on earth… the wealthiest country… the nation that drives the world's economy… the straw that stirs the drink. And you're saying we're broke? How can that be possible!

It's not *possible*. Not anymore. Possible means it *can* happen. It's too late for *can*. The deal is done. This ship has sailed. We're flat broke.

The United States of America has over $23 trillion in debt.

That's right, $23 *trillion*. A two, a one, a three, and twelve—count 'em, *twelve!*—zeros.

If you can't quite get a handle on that—or if your calculator doesn't go that far—try thinking about it in terms of billions.

The United States is $23 *thousand* billion in debt.

Still hard to grasp? Try this: $23 thousand thousand thousand thousand.

Have you ever actually sat down and thought about how much a trillion is? Imagine it in terms of a second, the time it takes to blink an eye.

Sixty seconds go by in a minute.

A thousand seconds go by in under seventeen minutes.

A trillion seconds go by in... wait for it... 31,709.8 years.

But hold on a second... That's just *one* trillion seconds. Twenty-three trillion seconds is 681,760.7 years. Now say that out loud: six hundred and eighty-one thousand, seven hundred and sixty years—and you still have about eight months left.

So here's what it means to have a $25 trillion debt.

If we slam on the brakes and bring it to a dead stop this very second and we begin paying the debt off at a dollar per second, we'll balance our books in the year 683,779.

Easy, right?

Nope. Because I said if we bring the debt to a dead stop *this very second*.

What was I thinking? What a ridiculous notion! The fact is our debt keeps growing—and not by just a little. We're digging our own grave, and we're doing a helluva job. That hole is getting hundreds of thousands of dollars deeper every second.

See for yourself. They even have a clock for that. Watch that debt grow, right here: www.USDebtClock.org/index.html.

* * *

What we have here is a failure to remunerate. We've created an unstoppable force that has to stop because—funny thing about debt—when folks loan you money, they kind of like to get paid back.

After a while, in fact, they start to demand it. Wait a little longer, and they start to get ornery. Keep kicking the can down the road, and things will get downright ugly.

Think about our nation's debt in personal terms.

Say you have a house and you can't pay your mortgage. The bank will give you a little time to get your house in order—but rest assured, it's not gonna tell you, "Everything's OK. We don't care. We don't want your money. Fuhgeddaboudit. Keep the house."

Or you're maxed out on your credit card, and you can't pay even the minimum balance when your statement arrives. Do you think the bank will smile, slap you on the back, offer you a beer, and raise your credit limit? Hell no, it won't. The bank will tell you, in no uncertain terms, that you need to cut that card up into itty-bitty pieces and then run it through your shredder a few times. It'll tell you that you can't charge so much as a pack of gum anymore. And, oh, pretty please, keep your phone with you at all times because our collections people would like to have a word with you.

Also, one more thing… please don't ask us about your old pals Equifax, Experian, and TransUnion—because we regret to inform you that your precious FICO score has just gone in the toilet. Want to borrow money to send your kid to college? Need a car loan? Planning a hard-earned and long-overdue vacation? Tough luck, pal.

That's what happens to people, and that's what's going to happen to the United States of America. And it's going to happen sooner than you think because we're up to our noses in debt, and we're sinking fast.

* * *

But... but... how did this happen? How did we do this to ourselves?

Well, friends, we did it the old-fashioned way: we worked really hard to earn a lot less and pay a lot more.

Consider this.

Sixty years ago, the maximum tax rate in the US was 90 percent.

No, that's not a typo. I said *90* percent. For every buck you made over $200,000, you got to pocket a dime. Your dear old Uncle Sam took the rest.

Of course, that 90 percent figure didn't sit very well with a lot of people who earned more than $200,000 at the time, including a sportscaster-turned-actor named Ronald Reagan. The idea that the government would take nine-tenths of his income offended him so much that he decided he would spend six months of the year making two movies—at $100,000 per movie—and the other six months running the Screen Actors Guild.

Reagan did very well as president of SAG—so well, in fact, that he decided he could be equally successful running something a little bigger, like the state of California. He became governor of the state in 1971 and served two terms, and then he nailed his audition for an even bigger role. He became president of the United States in 1981.

A major plank of Reagan's platform was an issue that's always popular among voters, one he knew well from his days as an actor: taxes.

Reagan said he'd cut them. And that's exactly what he did when he got into the White House. And that's pretty much what we've been doing ever since.

Today, the maximum tax rate in the US for every dollar earned over half a million dollars is less than 40 percent. If that sounds high, keep in mind that it used to be *90 percent.*

Everyone, across the board, is keeping more of their income today than they used to. And that would be wonderful and awesome, except for one tiny detail.

Taxes are our government's primary source of income. We've dramatically cut the government's income, and now we're broke. We're $23 trillion in debt and digging deeper into a hole every second of every day.

* * *

So, OK, we have a problem. We can do something about it, right?

Well, sure. It's easy. We can start by stopping spending. That's a great idea... right?

Well, maybe not. Not if you're a fan of, ummm, roads. And railways. And parks. Maybe not if you have a peculiar affinity for the army, navy, air force, marines, and coast guard. Maybe not if you think there's some value in having judges and police officers and teachers and air controllers and border patrollers and prison guards and forest rangers and members of Congress and the IRS and...

OK... maybe we can do without members of Congress and the IRS. But you get the idea.

There are a couple of other things that we pay lots of money for and that pretty much nobody wants to give up: Social Security and Medicare.

They're called entitlements and for good reason... we're entitled to them. Each and every one of us.

If you ever had a job, you set aside a small portion of your pay to buy into Medicare and Social Security. You did that—or you're in the process of doing that—for decades with the understanding that when your turn finally arrives, you'll be rightfully entitled to reap your reward.

When you turn sixty-five, I guarantee you'll want your Medicare card. And sometime between then and your seventieth birthday, I guarantee you'll want your Social Security check too.

You'll demand them—because you worked hard for forty-something years and you're entitled to them. I've yet to meet the man or woman who turned sixty-five and said, "That's OK. I don't want my money. You can keep it."

But there's a very sobering truth behind these entitlements.

Seventy-eight cents of every dollar the US government takes in goes right out for four things: Social Security, Medicare, Medicaid, and interest on the national debt.

And that number's going to go up, not down, soon because our demographics are shifting. We had a baby boom after World War II, and—*surprise!*—those babies are old and gray now.

We have more seniors than ever, and they're living longer than ever. Ten thousand people turn sixty-five *every day* in America, and that's going to keep happening for the next thirteen years.[2] And every one of those sixty-five-and-olders is going to get a Medicare card that guarantees them good, affordable medical care, courtesy of the American people.

---

2   Kristin Myers, "American Are Retiring at an Increasing Pace," Yahoo Finance, published November 21, 2018, https://finance.yahoo.com/news/americans-retiring-increasing-pace-145837368.html.

About 10,000 people retire every day, up from around 5,000 in 2000. Census projects this will rise to 12,000 per day

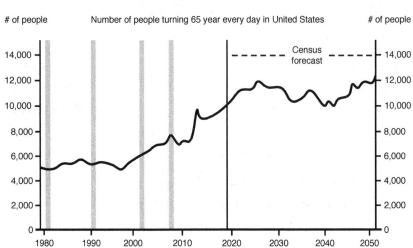

Source: US Census Bureau, Haver Analytic, DB Global Research, Nov 2018.

By the time they turn seventy-one, they'll be getting Social Security checks every month, too, because they're entitled to it. They played by the rules, and now it's their turn.

But there's a big problem with this system. The way it was designed, our senior citizens don't actually take out the money they put in. When money was withheld from their paychecks, it was used to provide Medicare and Social Security benefits for people who were sixty-five *then*. That's been the deal from the start: when you turn sixty-five, young folks will pay for your benefits just as you paid for old folks when you were young.

That seems fair enough, except… when all this started, there were more than forty-one workers in the US for every man or woman who retired.[3] In 2030 it will be two workers for every social security recipient.

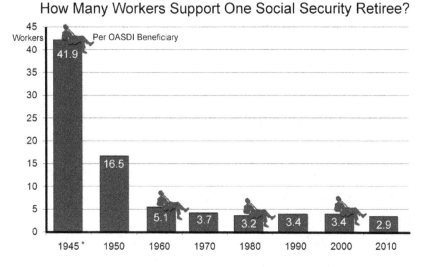

How Many Workers Support One Social Security Retiree?

Source: 2012 OASDI Trustee Report, Table IV.B2.,
www.ssa.gov, accessed May 21, 2012

And here's another inconvenient fact: Americans are having fewer children than they used to. In 2020 those over sixty-five will outnumber those under thirty—but those under thirty will still have to pay for the benefits of those over sixty-five.

It's as clear as can be: we're seeing increasingly fewer contributors and increasingly more recipients, and you don't need a doctorate in mathematics to know that this is unsustainable. It doesn't add up, and it's only going to get worse.

3   Veronique de Rugy, "How Many Workers Support One Social
    Security Retiree?" Mercatus Center, published May 22, 2012,
    https://www.mercatus.org/publications/government-spending/
    how-many-workers-support-one-social-security-retiree

* * *

The bottom line is this: we're going to be paying more money, and that means we're going to need more money to pay it. And the only way we're going to get more money is by taking it from our chief revenue source: us.

That's right... us.

Our government has made a whole bunch of promises it won't be able to keep unless it makes more money, and that money's going to have to come from... us.

We're over $23 trillion in debt, and we'll need to pay more for Medicare, Medicaid, and Social Security. And how do you think we're going to do that?

You probably know by now, but I'll tell you anyway.

We're going to raise taxes.

There's no two ways about it. This will not be a choice. Our government geniuses may invent clever ways to hide that fact, but you know what they say about putting lipstick on a pig... It's still a pig.

I'm sorry to inform you, but your taxes will be going up. Please don't shoot the messenger.

* * *

Now, let's be clear about something here. This isn't some cockamamie idea I had over a pepperoni pizza and a few six-packs.

But maybe you'd like a second opinion. Will David M. Walker do?

Walker was the US comptroller general—essentially the nation's CPA—for eleven years from 1998 through 2008. He was appointed by President Bill Clinton and kept his job through the administration of President George W. Bush. He's a registered Republican, but he's bipartisan when it comes to monitoring our money.

In 2008 Walker had a prominent role in the acclaimed documentary film *I.O.U.S.A*, which the film critic Roger Ebert said "accomplishes an amazing thing. It explains the national debt, the foreign trade deficit, the decrease in personal savings, how the prime interest rate works, and the weakness of our leaders... politicians of both parties, who know if they vote against tax cuts, they will be lambasted by their opponents and could lose their jobs."

The documentary was an eye-opener, but what I remember most was something Walker said and later repeated on a radio show I listened to.

Listen, he said, if you think that any political promise is going to change the way things are going to go, you're sadly mistaken. There is a four-letter word that will cripple our entire future.

Was that four-letter word *debt*?

That's a good one, but no.

Kids?

Another good one, but no.

Well then... what?

Math.

Math is crippling our country, Walker said. If you look at what we're spending compared to what we're taking in, it is unsustainable on any level, but we keep doing it anyway. It's like we can't help ourselves.

Need proof? Here's all the proof you need.

In 2008, when *I.O.U.S.A.* came out, the national debt was $9.6 trillion. Now, just ten years later, it has more than doubled. It's $23 trillion. And what do we do about it? How do we deal with this?

We raise our debt limit every damn time. We raise it because we can't stay within it—but every time we do it, we're defying math. We're slapping Band-Aids on a severed artery. We look better—but underneath, we're bleeding to death. "Band-Aids don't fix bullet holes," said Taylor Swift… OK, maybe she is good.

* * *

> We raise our debt limit every damn time. We raise it because we can't stay within it—but every time we do it, we're defying math.

Here's another thing David M. Walker, America's CPA, said.

Tax rates will have to go up—and not by just a little. The United States is insolvent, and taxes will have to *double* if we want to meet our expenditures.

So say hello to Hurricane Destitution, our first and biggest looming storm. The government needs more revenue, American taxpayers will have to provide it, and that means a tax hike—a big tax hike—is coming our way.

And *that* brings us back to our tax-deferred retirement accounts: our 401(k)s and IRAs.

I'll bet you have one. And if you do, I'll bet you remember that they advised you to stash as much of your income into it as you could afford because you wouldn't pay taxes on that income until you retired and started to withdraw it.

And I'll bet you remember that they said this would be great because your tax bracket would be lower when the time came to start withdrawing the money you saved.

Now maybe you also remember a scene near the end of the movie *Animal House*, where Otter tells Flounder, "You f***ed up... you trusted us!"

Well, guess what. They lied to you. Your tax bracket won't be lower.

They were lying, and you f***ed up. You trusted them.

* * *

If someone had hired me to tell the government how to fix its problems, that's exactly the kind of lie I'd have told it to spin. I'd have said, "Let's create a savings investment scheme and tell people, 'Hey, you'll be in a lower tax bracket when you retire! Why pay taxes now when you can defer paying them until later? You'll be better off putting your money into a 401(k) or an IRA, sitting back, and watching it grow.'"

That's what I would have said, but they didn't need my advice. They figured it out all by themselves. It sounded great, and it's exactly what they did.

But they were lying.

Here's what really happened.

You planted a seed, and you got a tax break on it. And over time, that seed grew into a big oak tree. And now you have to pay taxes on that oak tree.

And maybe you were in the 15 percent bracket when you planted that seed. Maybe you were getting a weekly paycheck, and being oh so smart and very frugal, you managed to put $100 of your pay into a 401(k) each and every week. At the end of the year, you had $5,200 in that account and you felt like the king of the world—because you got out of paying the government $780. And you went out for a nice dinner and told your date you were the smartest guy on earth.

But guess what? You married that girl, and now you're in the 37 percent bracket, and the time has come to start withdrawing from your 401(k), and every time you take out $100, you have to pay the government thirty-seven bucks. Pull out $5,200 now, and the government will skim $1,924 right off the top.

And now your spouse is starting to think that maybe you weren't as smart as you said you were.

But wait a minute. Have you forgotten what I told you? Did you forget I said the government is going to raise your taxes? How do you think your spouse will feel if you're in the 50 percent or 60 percent tax bracket?

I'll tell you how she'll feel... She'll feel lousy. But it's on you. Those geniuses assured you your tax bracket would be lower, but it's not going to happen. They were lying.

And you f***ed up. You trusted them.

* * *

Here's another thing you may not have fully understood when you set up your retirement account. They probably weren't very forthcoming in telling you this, but you had alternatives. Nobody forced you to do what you did.

What do you think you might have done if they'd told you that the government doesn't really know a whole lot about what you own? Your local government knows the value of your home—but the feds don't. They also don't know if you own vintage cars, cabinets full of old 33 rpm records, a vault filled with furs, or diamonds or gold or a collection of pristine-condition baseball cards signed by Hall of Famers.

They don't know any of that... but they know every minuscule detail of your 401(k) or your IRA or your 403(b) or your 457s because you have to report the status of those accounts to the IRS every year.

In fact, that's why you're not even allowed to have custody of your own account. It's held by a custodian who has to tell the government exactly what's in it every year.

Now think about that for a minute. If you own shares in Taco Bell, the government knows nothing—except how much you receive in dividends. But if you have a 401(k), it knows everything.

And why should you care what the government knows?

Here's why: our government is $23 trillion in debt. And right now, as I'm writing this, Americans have $34 trillion in their retirement accounts.

That's two ledgers—one drowning in red ink, the other flush with black. And do you think for even a second that when our debt crisis hits DEFCON 1 the government won't take a hard look at that $34 trillion and see a way out of this mess? Do you think they won't look for a way to move a whole pile of zeros from one ledger to the other?

If you don't, you're nuts. Because they will. You can bet the farm on it.

In fact, they've already figured some of this out. If you have a 401(k) or an IRA, you are required by law to start pulling out a minimum distribution every year, based on how much you have in your account, as soon as you turn seventy and a half years old.

You have to pay income taxes on that distribution, of course, and you certainly want to—because they'll slap a 50 percent penalty on you if you don't.

Your government has made damn sure that it will be receiving what amounts to an annuity from your account every year, beginning no later than six months after your seventieth birthday. Your Uncle Sam thanks you for your generosity.

And here's something your Uncle Sam knows very well: there's a lot more money where that annuity came from—and he's broke.

Do you really think he won't come knocking on your door, looking for more?

Of course, he will—because it's simple math. He owes $23 trillion. You have $34 trillion. Once you're seventy and a half, you'll have to start making withdrawals and paying taxes on what you withdraw. And the higher your tax rate, the more you'll pay.

You don't need a slide rule to figure this one out.

* * *

But wait, you say. You're really smart, and you can win this game yet. You've done so well that you don't need the money in that account. You'll withdraw the absolute minimum required by law and pay taxes on it, but you won't touch the rest of your stash—and when you and your spouse have left the ballpark for good, everything will go to your kids and grandkids.

Sure, they'll have to pay a large chunk of taxes on it, but you'll still have left them a wonderful gift to remember you by.

Right?

Ummm… maybe not.

There's a line of thinking that's being bandied about, and it goes like this.

If you and your spouse have left money in a tax-deferred account such as a 401(k) or an IRA when you die, why should that money be treated the same as money you leave in a savings or checking account?

You never paid any taxes on the money in that 401(k), so it really should be put into a special tax bracket—say, 60 percent or even more. And the government can skim that right off the top before whatever's left gets distributed to your survivors.

Does that sound horrifying? Do you think it's unfathomable that the government would even consider confiscating 60 percent of the money you leave in your 401(k) for your kids and grandkids?

It sounds horrifying to me, but I can see the logic.

The money in that account was *your* retirement money, and you chose not to use it before you died. Your spouse didn't use it either, and well… why and how is that different from a pension?

If you have a pension, your payments end when you and your spouse die. Now why should the money you leave in your 401(k) be any different? No one made you defer those taxes. No one put a gun to your head. You could have put it in anything you wanted, and you chose a tax-deferred retirement account.

It was there for *you*, not for your kids. You didn't get around to taking out all the money you put in—but so what? If you'd had a pension, the payments would have dried up when you did. So why should your 401(k) automatically pass on to your kids—especially when your government is broke and this is an easy and logical source it can tap?

Your Uncle Sam thanks you very much. Again.

Now, they can call this whatever they want, but I call it confiscation of wealth. Socialism, communism, pure, plain, and simple.

But who cares what I think? Who cares what *you* think? Our government—the left *and* the right—is thinking about all of this because it's broke and it needs your money.

It just hasn't quite figured out how to sell it yet. But believe me, it will.

* * *

Look, taxes are a part of life. If you like driving on pavement… if you like being protected by people in uniform… then you understand that it takes money to pay for those things, and that money has to come from you.

But how you provide that money—and how much you provide—is still up to you. There are decisions you can make that will help you control that money flow. They're not easy decisions, but for the time being, they're still yours to make.

You need a plan. Not the government's plan... *your* plan. Because the government's plan sucks. It sucks for you, your spouse, your kids, your grandkids. If you have goldfish, it sucks for them too. The government's plan is best for the government, not for you.

Don't ever forget that the government's broke, and it wants—and *needs*—every dollar it can take from you.

So don't make it easier for them. While you still have time, develop a plan that's tailor-made just for you, a plan that lets you keep as much of your money as possible out of the government's hands.

Maybe that means biting the bullet and paying taxes now—so you may never have to pay taxes again. Maybe that means investing in stocks or bonds or real estate or all or none of the above.

Maybe you don't like your tax rate now, but who's to say it won't be worse in the future? Do you want to make decisions based on hopes and dreams, or do you want to make them based on facts, understandable logic, and true strategies to succeed? If you pay your taxes today, you're basing your decision on a fact, not a hope. You're building a foundation in stone instead of building it in the sand and hoping the tide won't come in.

Because trust me on this... the tide always comes in.

* * *

When all is said and done, you want to invest in a low-tax environment. You want to keep what you earned. And you can.

You have lots of options—provided you're not content to sit around and do nothing. Keep doing that, and I promise you… the government will make your choice for you.

I'll promise you one more thing: if you let the government choose, you'll end up wishing you hadn't.

The last time I looked, this was still the land of the free. So why not choose freely while you still can? Your decisions won't be easy ones, but at least they'll be yours.

If you wait too long, though, they won't be. Hurricane Destitution is lapping at our shores, and taxes will be going up—and by a lot—very soon.

That storm is coming. You can deal with it when it smashes through your doors and windows and floods your home, or you can prepare—*now!*—to flee to higher ground or ride it out.

But you can't afford to stick your head in the sand and keep putting things off because this isn't the only storm on the horizon. There are others out there, heading our way, destined to join it.

See the video at
www.StormproofRetirement.com/perfectstorm

CHAPTER FOUR

Storm No. 2

We're Buying Crap on Credit

America. What a country! You can get everything from a candy bar to a car to a condo—even if you don't have a penny in your pocket.

All you need is a credit card. How awesome is that?

Well, really, it's not as awesome as it sounds.

Getting stuff with credit is great for the good ol' GDP—that gross domestic product they keep talking about on the business news reports—because the more we get, the more we need to produce.

It's great for American consumers too. Who on earth doesn't want to get pretty much whatever he wants whenever he wants it?

But it isn't great for America.

Getting stuff with credit is *horrible* for America because... did you notice that I've been saying "get," not "buy"? I haven't said "buy" because we aren't really buying the stuff we get.

Most of the time, we're getting stuff without paying for it. We're using credit instead of dead presidents—and the more we lay down plastic instead of greenbacks, the greater the odds we'll never save enough money to pay off what we owe.

We're awash in credit, and pretty soon we'll be drowning in it. This is our storm no. 2—Tropical Storm MasterVisa. It's heading our way, all set to collide with storm no. 1. And when it does, there'll be hell to pay.

* * *

Consumer spending accounts for 68 percent of the US economy.[4] When we're not spending, the economy isn't growing. When the economy isn't growing, businesses go bust. And nobody wants that—so we do everything we can to keep our economy humming, no matter the cost.

We do it by offering credit.

Don't have a hundred bucks for groceries? Use your credit card.

Don't have money for a new car? Here's a six-year loan.

Don't have $300,000 to send your kid to a four-year college? Here's a student loan.

Credit is more addictive than nicotine and as habit forming as crack, and we're hooked on it. We start mainlining before we're even old enough to drink.

We send our kids to college, and the first person they meet is a nice man or woman offering them a piece of plastic just waiting to have their name embossed on it. It has a beautiful photo of their campus and an EMV chip on the front, a magnetic strip on the back, and a credit limit that's just begging to be raised.

---

4   Kimberly Amadeo, "Consumer Spending Trends and Current Statistics," Balance, updated November 1, 2019, https://www.thebalance.com/consumer-spending-trends-and-current-statistics-3305916.

Sign up now, kids, and we'll throw in a T-shirt!

And then they're hooked too. Just like Mom and Dad.

* * *

The average American has 2.6 credit cards. Take out the 29 percent of Americans who don't have any, and that number jumps to 3.7.[5]

Some give you cash back on every purchase. Others give you travel points. You can fly around the world for "free"—maybe even in first class—on the points you accumulate using your card.

Those perks make you feel so good, you just might forget how much debt you took on to earn them—not to mention the 95 to 995 bucks you pay every year just for the card.[6]

But even if you don't have a credit card, you still could be drowning in credit debt.

I'll bet you have a car or two or even more if you have kids. Do you really own your car? Did you actually buy it—or did you take out a loan to "get" it?

What's the interest on that loan? Do you even know?

If you could have bought your car for, say, $40,000—do you know how much more it's going to cost you to pay off a car loan, with interest, over four, five, or six years?

What's that? You actually *do* own your car? Good for you. Next question...

Do you own a home?

Really? Do you actually own it... or are you paying off a mortgage?

---

5   Ascent Staff, "How Many Credit Cards Does the Average Person Have?," Ascent, published November 15, 2018, https://www.fool.com/the-ascent/credit-cards/articles/how-many-credit-cards-does-the-average-person-have/.

6   Linsey Knerl, "15 of the World's Most Exclusive Credit Cards," CardRates.com, updated April 4, 2019, https://www.cardrates.com/advice/most-exclusive-credit-cards/.

OK, maybe you don't have a mortgage. Maybe you really do own your home. Do you know what'll happen next? It won't be long before someone from the bank calls you on the phone and tells you that you're sitting on dead equity. It's just lying there, doing nothing.

So how about putting that equity to some use? If you get a home equity line, you can use it to... buy stuff!

You can go to the Super Bowl... you can cruise around the world on the *Queen Mary*. With a large equity line, you might even be able to buy tickets to see the Rolling Stones.

And you know what? You'll do it. Because if there's one thing everyone has told you, it's that owning a home is better than having money in the bank. The value of your home will go up, guaranteed. It never goes down. That's how real estate works.

So why not take out a loan against the equity in your home and use the money to buy some playthings? Why stick with a Camry when you can drive a Lexus? Why vacation in Missouri when you can be in Maui? Just borrow some money, and pay it off later. What's the harm?

Here's the harm: credit is fake wealth. It allows us to spend four to six times more than we actually earn. And since the average American lives paycheck to paycheck, that's a recipe for economic disaster.

> Here's the harm: credit is fake wealth. It allows us to spend four to six times more than we actually earn.

* * *

Consider for a moment the risks of living paycheck to paycheck. If you have nothing saved, what are you going to do if you lose your job? What the hell are you going to do when you want to retire? What if you get sick?

Now think about how much worse things will be if your paycheck disappears and you're saddled with credit debt.

Seriously, now… we have all these people living paycheck to paycheck, using credit to buy stuff. What's going to happen when they want to retire… or when they have no choice in the matter?

Ten thousand Americans turn sixty-five every day, and on average they've saved less than $40,000. That means that every day, thousands of Americans hit the trifecta from hell: no savings, a monthly Social Security check that doesn't cover their expenses, and considerable credit card debt that they've acquired over the years.

Now what?

They'll either have to work until the day they die—which might not come for another thirty years or so, since we're living much longer than we were when Social Security became our social safety net…

Or we'll have to create another social safety net. Those of us who saved well will have to use our money to bail them out.

And that's exactly what we'll do. Sure, we'll resent it because every dollar we give them will be a dollar we can't give to ourselves.

But it will be hard to put the blame on them. They did exactly what we told them to do: they bought crap with credit.

But wait… it gets worse. Except for health care, those senior citizens will be consuming less. They won't be buying cars every couple of years. They won't be taking long vacations. They'll be buying less expensive clothing and eating in fewer restaurants.

They won't do our economy any good at all.

So here's the bottom line: we're screwed.

* * *

We got a preview of this mess just a decade ago.

Do you remember it? It was called the Great Recession.

A lot of people lost their jobs in 2008, and they suddenly couldn't pay the bills they'd piled up when they bought stuff with credit instead of cash. The banks didn't want to make a bad situation worse, so they stopped offering credit. And since we couldn't get credit, we stopped spending. Some of us stopped because we didn't have as much money as we did in 2007. The rest of us stopped because we couldn't get more credit.

But all of us were affected. Even if you'd paid off your mortgage and actually owned your home, you couldn't get a home equity loan to reshingle your roof—because that's what happens when the banks suddenly cut off credit. The roof leaks.

And it's starting to leak again. That rumble you hear in the distance is thunder. A big storm is coming, and we're not ready for it. Consumer debt is actually higher today than it was in 2007, the year before the meltdown. It's like we learned nothing in 2008.

But it's not our fault. We've just been doing what our government and its partner in crime—the banks—want us to do. They want us to use our credit cards, to take out home equity loans, to "buy" new cars with no money down and six years to pay even when our old cars are working just fine.

We're offering you a fabulous low interest rate, dude. Now get out there and *spend*! Keep buying crap on credit. You'll get the stuff you want—even if you don't need it—and you'll keep the economy moving!

You can pay us back later. No problem.

* * *

Now here's what they don't tell you: read the fine print. Know what you're getting into.

You'll have to make payments every month. But don't worry… you don't have to pay a lot. You owe us $8,000 now, but your minimum payment the first month will be only 80 bucks, and that's all we really want from you. Pay that minimum every month, and we'll reward you with a fabulous credit score.

Oh, by the way… we'll be charging you interest at an outrageous rate on every cent you carry over. But just keep paying that minimum every month, and everything will be paid off in twenty-three years, at which point you'll have paid $19,000. But that isn't too long or too much when you consider how low your monthly payments were, right?

Wrong. But that's OK because it probably won't go down that way. They won't let you stop at $8,000. They'll let you borrow even more crap on that card until you hit your credit limit. And when you do, they'll be delighted to raise that limit because you're a very good customer and they want you to be able to buy even more crap and owe them even more money.

But sooner or later—probably sooner—you'll hit that limit again and again, until the day finally comes when they say it's enough. No more credit for you, dude. You're maxed out. Now pay the damn bill.

What's that? You desperately need money to pay for something you truly need? Too bad. The well's gone dry. Now pay the damn bill.

You don't have the money? OK, we'll put you in touch with the folks at our collection agency. We pay them to be unpleasant. They'll make your life miserable until you pay your bill… or go bankrupt. Up to you.

And there you have it—the scenario from hell. It's not only going to happen in the future, it's happening now. And it's just going to get worse because we're compiling too much debt and we can't keep increasing production forever.

* * *

Here's what's crazy about all of this: we brought it on ourselves.

We're consumers. We spend and spend to keep everything humming. We have met the enemy, and he is us.

Think about it... Who keeps a 1998 Toyota Camry, even if it's running perfectly? Who gallivants around town in one, showing it off because it's paid off? Admit it... Don't you feel a bit jealous of that guy driving the Lexus or the Beemer or the Escalade or even the brand-new Camry with all those bells and whistles they didn't have in 1998? Isn't it time you upgraded from CD to Bluetooth? From cruise control to self-steering?

Of course, it's time! All you have to do is sign a couple pieces of paper and make payments for a few years. C'mon, you know you want it.

We don't even buy a $1,000 refrigerator with cash anymore. We use a credit card, or we get in-store credit. If we don't pay it off immediately or within the prescribed three-month limit, they'll charge us 27 percent interest, but hey... that ice dispenser works great, doesn't it?

* * *

Our mind-numbing dependence on personal credit pretty much began back in the late sixties or early seventies, when banks started saying, "We'll lend you a lot more to buy that house because that house will be an appreciating asset."

When it dawned on them that you'd probably be in your home for only eight or nine years, they created the concept of amortization tables. They decided to front-load all their fees so you'd pay very little principal in the first ten years of a thirty-year mortgage.

But since that meant you'd still owe most of your principal after a decade, they had to find a way to make it sound attractive. So they went to the federal government and asked, "Hey, how can we make people buy this?"

And our government found a way to help. It decided to let us deduct those front-loaded interest payments from our taxable income.

Why did the government do this? To increase the GDP.

If you could deduct your mortgage interest from your taxable income, you'd pay less in taxes, leaving more money in your pocket that you could use to… go out and buy stuff.

Armed with this impeccable logic, our government decided to help banks propagate the myth that buying on credit—and raising your personal debt—was a good thing.

They did the same thing with student loans. Except for our military academies, we have no federal university—but the government controls every student loan obtained with federal funding. It helps generate hundreds of billions of dollars in revenues for the banks every year, providing them with more money they can use to finance even more things.

So the government wants us to buy crap on credit. It helps the banks, and the banks help the government. They give you money to spend that actually belongs to other people, and they make it clear that if you don't pay them back, they'll make your life miserable.

But they really don't want to do that. They'd much rather just increase your interest rate—because they know that if there's one thing you truly fear, it's the thought of going bankrupt. They know that come hell or high water, you'll find a way to pay them what you owe them before you'll let yourself declare bankruptcy.

It's legal racketeering—kind of like the Mafia, only no thumbs get broken. The only reason racketeering is illegal is because the government can't get a piece of the pie. Think about it... If loan sharks agreed to pay the government a reasonable slice of what they collect in "interest," would the government want to put them out of business?

Credit keeps our nation running. That's an inescapable fact. Without credit, our country doesn't grow, and that has a cascading effect.

No economic growth means no real wage growth, which means companies don't make more money and the stock market doesn't go up.

And that makes us feel bad—even if we have no money in the stock market.

But why? If we're debt-free, totally solvent, and have no skin in the game, why do we feel bad when there's no growth on Wall Street?

It's because we feel like we've been invited to a party and the punch bowl is empty.

* * *

When you take away credit, you have an empty punch bowl—and nobody likes an empty punch bowl. That's why the government has not only been refilling it since 2008, it's been letting it overflow.

But sooner or later—and if I were you, I'd bet on sooner—it has to end. We're going to run out of punch. And when we do, everyone's going to hit the road in search of an after-party.

And even if we don't run with that crowd, we'll be sharing the highway with the people who do. They shouldn't be behind the wheel, but they're driving anyway—and that means a whole lot of us, no matter how sober, will wind up colliding head on with them.

And we're going to get hurt because our government always bails out those of us who don't do well.

Consider Social Security. We didn't create it for people who saved well. We invented it for people who lived too long and used up all their money. Now, do you think our government won't keep doing that?

I promise you, it will. The only question is how.

We've already seen one way: our progressive tax system. The more you earn, the higher your tax bracket. The more you save, the more the government takes. It's a system that's worked for almost a century.

But what's going to happen if everything crashes? Who's going to bail us out? What if, just as in 2008, people who took out NINJA[7] loans to buy houses they really couldn't afford suddenly can't make their monthly payments?

Here's what will happen: we, the responsible ones, will pay for it.

We'll pay for it even if they don't raise our taxes because when credit disappears, the stock market will probably tank—and take us down with it. Whether we drank the punch or not, we'll be wobbling.

We'll bail out the undersavers in our midst because our systems have evolved to cater to the weakest. We're Americans; we help those who need help. We don't throw the meth addicts over the cliff; we try to help them clean up and get straight. It's what we do.

And we also understand that to a certain degree, we're responsible for their irresponsibility. It's easy to criticize those who undersaved, but let's not forget that we encouraged them to do it. We all helped build our credit-based economy.

---

7   NINJA loans are loans taken out by people with no income, no job, or no assets.

Our government and our banking system encouraged wild abuses of credit over the last half century, and very soon almost all of us will pay dearly for their recklessness. We're going to crash—unless we plan correctly.

> Our government and our banking system encouraged wild abuses of credit over the last half century, and very soon almost all of us will pay dearly for their recklessness.

We need to install guardrails on the highways and airbags in our cars so that if a punch-drunk driver hits us, we don't go tumbling off the side of the mountain with him.

We need to make sure we survive. It may be uncomfortable, but we'll live to drive again.

* * *

Here's what bothers me most about this credit mess.

We wouldn't even be having this discussion if we still had pensions. When we stopped giving people pensions—when we reduced payments or changed how they worked—nobody bothered to tell us how those changes would affect our lives.

They took away our safety nets and started promoting a credit industry that they said would keep the economy going, but nobody told us how important it was to maintain a savings account and put money into it every week. I don't recall anyone flinging a federal or state manual across the table and saying, "Read this in your spare time."

We thought, "Oh, you know, Social Security will be fine." And yes, it might have been—if only we'd remembered to die before we hit the age of seventy.

But what if you didn't? What if you were born in 1950, when you had a life expectancy of sixty-eight, and you forgot to die in 2018?

Here's what: when you turn seventy in 2020, you'll have a new life expectancy. It'll be eighty-five if you're a man, eighty-seven and a half if you're a woman. In fact, if you turn seventy in 2020, there's a one-in-four chance you'll live past ninety and a one-in-ten chance you'll see one hundred.

So here you are, all set to retire at sixty-five, and you're suddenly and very unexpectedly saying to yourself, "Oh, crap! I've been working for forty-five years, ever since I was twenty, and now you're telling me I might still be around in thirty years?

"What am I supposed to live on? Social Security? I paid to raise a family, put braces on my kids' teeth, sent them off to college, paid for a wedding or two, bought a house… and now you're telling me I should have saved lots of money on top of all that to pay my way through thirty years of retirement?"

Do you recall ever having a conversation about this? I sure don't. I have three master's degrees, and I never heard a word about this in any of the MBA or financial classes I attended. And I know why.

It's because all of this was a big experiment, and the baby boomers, the ones who are turning sixty-five every day now, were the guinea pigs. Their parents had pensions, they kept their money in banks, and they didn't buy stuff on credit. They grew up during the Great Depression, and if there was one thing they knew, it was how to say, "I don't have money. I'm not buying that."

All that and they died younger too.

But they changed the game for the baby boomers—and they didn't bother to tell them the new rules. They told them to fill the tank with credit debt, put the pedal to the metal, and head out on the highway. Nobody said there'd be switchbacks and hairpin curves.

They also created a climate where it feels important to stay one step ahead of the Joneses. So even if you have $1 million in savings, you may still be up to your neck in credit debt.

Let's say you've made a ton of money, and you have a McMansion in a great neighborhood. I'll bet you have a large mortgage on it—and I'll bet you don't want to leave it when you retire.

I don't know anyone who ever said, "OK, I'm a corporate executive, I'm a doctor, I'm a lawyer, I'm a financial person, and I have a nine-thousand-square-foot home with a helicopter pad, two tennis courts, and a swimming pool—and I'm just going to leave them all behind and move to a one-bedroom apartment when I retire because I've done a poor job saving."

Nope. Not gonna happen. You'll take advantage of all the credit you can get your hands on to stay just where you are. Credit may not affect you as much as it affects most of us, but it's still going to have an impact.

* * *

At the end of the day, when all is said and done, we're in a looming crisis because our government did everything it could to help banks make more money. That benefited all of us in some ways because buying stuff on credit pushed the markets up and built a flourishing economy.

But that benefit isn't sustainable at our current debt level.

We have more debt than ever, more than we had before the 2008 crash. We borrowed to the hilt and paid interest to the banks—so much that they could put a branch building on just about every corner.

They've been double-dipping, getting money from the government and, thanks to credit, from us. And they've herded us into debt.

They made us believe our lives would be enriched if only we got that new fridge, that double oven, that super-duper digital display washer-and-dryer combo we didn't really need, but we really, really wanted.

They took us down a primrose path of purchases they told us would fulfill our lives—and we fell for it.

We could have said, "Those are expensive, honey. We shouldn't buy them. We don't have the money."

But we didn't. What we said instead was "It's OK, honey. We've got plastic."

The banks, helped by our government, did this to us. And now everything's going to come crashing down on our heads. I can't say exactly when, but it's coming. And soon.

You can take that to the bank.

* * *

Now, maybe you haven't fallen into that sinkhole. Maybe you're one of the lucky few who always pay with cash, put aside a slice of their paychecks every week, and are marching toward their retirement years with zero debt.

If you're one of them... congratulations. You're not part of the problem.

That's the good news. Now here's the bad.

You're going to be part of the solution. We're going to need your money to prop up all those other folks who got caught up in the game.

The earth is shaking. There's a credit tsunami heading our way. And don't think for a New York minute that you'll be able to watch it from higher ground.

It will flood your home and wash away your car. You may not drown, but you're going to get very wet—unless you're guaranteed a steady income on top of your Social Security that will keep you comfortable for the rest of your life.

Something that's kind of like… a pension.

I have people come into my office for retirement planning who have practically nothing in the bank—but they have a pension waiting in the wings for the day they stop working, one that will pay them a nice sum of money every month for the rest of their lives.

They come in and say, "Jon, we make only five grand a month, but we spend only two. Are we OK?"

And I tell them, "You're good. You need to earmark some of those pension payments for health care and maybe something for the kids when you're gone. But other than that, you're in awesome shape. You nailed it."

As long as those pensions stay solvent—as long as that check comes in every month for the rest of their lives—they'll be fine.

They prepared for the tsunami.

But did you? If you're not sure, then you better hurry up and get sure.

First and foremost, you need to get a handle on how much debt you really have. And don't lie to yourself. You need to know what your budget will look like if you don't have access to credit because that will dictate everything you do.

Should you pay off your home before you retire? Should you get rid of the lake house? What will happen to your savings if interest rates go up… or down?

You need to know exactly where you're standing before you can decide where you want to go.

Think about the road ahead. You'll be more comfortable if it's smoothly paved, with strong guardrails and streetlamps. You want to be riding in a solid car with good tires, great crash ratings, and the best airbags because you may encounter a deer in the road or a big pothole or a kid who's too busy texting to see you in his high beams.

You need to know what lies ahead—and what can go wrong—so you can be ready for anything.

A big credit storm is coming. Interest rates are going to rise—and when they do, a lot of people won't be able to make their payments.

And there's a cherry on top of this sundae: college loans.

We have millions of kids coming out of college with no tangible skills to make them attractive to potential employers, and they're up to their necks in college loans.

The government's on the hook for those loans, and there's just no way it's going to hold those kids' feet to the fire and demand payment—because they're kids.

They didn't see what might happen, and we certainly didn't help them. We told them to take the loans and go to the best college they couldn't afford. We didn't encourage their parents to say, "You know, you can go to a very good school that doesn't cost seventy-five thousand dollars a year, and you'll still be able to get your teaching certificate. We want you do well, but let's be realistic."

We chose fantasy over reality. We said, "Don't worry about it. Just take out a loan. Trust us, you'll be fine."

Well, we're not going to be fine—even if we didn't play the game. Because if lots of people go bankrupt, the government will still have to stay in business. And since it can't squeeze blood from a turnip... since it won't raise taxes on people who have no money to pay them... it will have to get its money from another source: the rest of us.

It'll come after our 401(k)s, our 403(b)s, our IRAs. It will come after those tax-deferred savings plans because it will have no choice.

So be prepared for it. Have a plan. And have a contingency plan on top of that plan.

A famous philosopher named Mike Tyson once said, "Everybody has a plan until they get punched in the face."

Don't ever forget that. If you know that left hook is coming, if you know you're going to get punched in the face, then learn how to duck. And while you're at it, learn how to avoid the right uppercut that's coming next.

Be prepared for the fight because you want to make sure the arm the referee raises when it's over is yours. It's really important because this isn't the only storm that's heading your way.

You need to be in good shape to fight the next one too.

See the video on debt at
www.StormproofRetirement.com/debt

CHAPTER FIVE

Storm No. 3

They're Selling Us Junk

B y now you're probably soaked to the bone and standing knee deep in a rising flood.

But don't get too comfortable: there are new clouds forming on the horizon.

Storm no. 3 is on the way.

It's all the junk—that's right, *junk*—we've got in our retirement portfolios.

If you're like most folks, you've chosen one of four places to stash your savings. The first one is under your mattress, which really isn't as bad as it sounds. Mattress accounts guarantee that you won't lose your savings in a major economic downturn. They provide good back support too.

But mattress accounts also have a downside. They dramatically increase your risk of total loss in the event of a robbery or a fire or a hungry dog or an unsavory houseguest. If you stash all your money under your mattress and come home to discover that it's not there anymore, there's no FMIC—Federal Mattress Insurance Corporation—to protect you.

So on balance, we don't recommend mattress savings.

This leaves most of us with three remaining avenues for saving: insurance companies, banks, and Wall Street. And if there's one thing we all know, because it's what we've been hearing our entire lives, it's that only one of these—Wall Street—can make us rich.

Right?

Wrong. They've been telling us this since forever, but they've been lying.

They've been selling us junk, not unlike an exercise machine on a TV infomercial: *Buy the Ab Cruncher 4700 Six-Pack, and you'll have abs of steel!*

Well, maybe—if we use the contraption every day, exactly as instructed, as part of a larger workout regime, combined with a low-carb diet and so on. And just in case, they always put a disclaimer at the end in small type and spoken very fast: *These results are not typical. Not all people end up with perfect washboard abs.* Let's get real. We know how this ends—there'll be an Ab Cruncher 4700 Six-Pack collecting dust in our closet.

That's exactly how it is with the market funds Wall Street says are our tickets to wealth. If we don't invest well and monitor our savings meticulously—and the odds are very good that we won't—we'll wind up going nowhere fast.

Chew on this for a minute: if putting our money into Wall Street mutual funds is the greatest way to build wealth, how come there aren't hundreds of millions of millionaires tooling around out there in their Lamborghinis?

Here's why.

It's because Wall Street lied. It sold us a lovely sounding bill of goods, and most of us bought it.

If you're like most people who work for a living, you've been setting aside a slice of every paycheck and socking it into a tax-free IRA or 401(k). You've been doing it diligently, putting the money into one Wall Street investment fund or another. But there's a sobering fact that nobody's told you until now: you've been putting that money into junk.

Wall Street shrewdly offered to sell you junk, and you went ahead and bought it.

* * *

Now, I know what you're thinking. How can this be? What are you talking about?

Well, think about this for a minute. What exactly does Wall Street create?

The answer is nothing. Wall Street creates nothing.

It provides no service. It manufactures nothing you can put your hands on.

Here's what Wall Street does. It takes money from one person, finds a way to slap a fee on it internally, and sells it to someone else.

Our nation's biggest and best investment firms have succeeded beyond their wildest dreams at taking our money and making an immense amount of money off it without producing even a single tangible product.

They've created a giant cash machine and hooked us up to it, and all they have to do now is keep it humming.

The people at the top of our nation's financial services industry have figured out that it's a lot easier to make money from internal fees and trading costs than from anything they could actually produce.

That's what Wall Street does. It makes money. That's its sole purpose.

But there's a problem with all of this. Wall Street doesn't make money for you and me. The only ones it makes real money for are the people who control it.

> Wall Street doesn't make money for you and me. The only ones it makes real money for are the people who control it.

The system isn't exactly rigged—there's nothing maniacal about all of this because nobody actually forced us to put our money into the market. But the truth is undeniable: we, the investors, aren't the ones who are getting rich.

Here's something else that's true. We bought into this willingly because Wall Street succeeded in shifting our mind-set from one that honored sensible saving to one that promotes "informed" gambling.

And it did it very well—so well, in fact, that it essentially controls our entire economy.

It has the good-government seal of approval too. Our leaders have gone all in on this because whatever money we make in the market they can tax the hell out of.

But here's where we've gone wrong: Wall Street is making a hell of a lot of money off our money and most of us don't have a clue how much.

* * *

I have a simple question for you.

How's your broker doing? Is he really working for you?

I'm sure you're investing with a reputable brokerage house, and there's nothing inherently wrong with that. But if that brokerage has shareholders—and I'll bet the farm that it does—then I promise you, your broker isn't putting you first.

You're not the one he has to please. You're just his profit center.

If he wants to keep his job—if he wants to keep his summer home and his sailboat and buy his wife that nice Mercedes he promised her—if he's *smart*, he's concentrating on his shareholders' happiness. Not yours.

What's that you say? You don't have a broker. You have a financial advisor.

Ummmm... not really. If you think a financial advisor isn't a broker, you're probably wrong. Ditto if you have a wealth advisor or a wealth planner or a private wealth orchestrator or a financial consultant...

There are countless titles, so take your pick. They go by whatever sounds good—but 98 percent of them are brokers.

Now, that doesn't mean brokers are inherently bad. There's nothing unethical about earning a commission. But know this... No matter what your broker calls himself, there's something he's not telling you.

He's really a well-compensated salesman whose job is to pitch you a suitable product that you can buy legally.

And that can pose a problem because that suitable product isn't necessarily what's best for you. If you're happy, that's great—but your happiness isn't what really matters. Your broker's main interest is very different from yours. His main interest, the one that keeps him in business, is making the shareholders happy. You will always come in second. Now, what happens if your best interests don't match your broker's? Whose do you think will prevail?

I'll give you a hint: your broker loves his job, and he wants to keep it.

His shareholders always come first, and they focus on one thing and one thing only: profit. The brokerage house always chooses profit over people. You can take that to the bank.

* * *

The choice of profit over people explains why brokers are constantly offering us a variety of financial products to invest in. They know that the more we shift our money around, the more the shareholders can skim off the top.

And how much is that? The sky's the limit. Go to New York or Chicago and look at all the skyscrapers they've built. Step inside, and be dazzled by those spectacular marble floors. Go back outside, and envy their fancy cars.

And now that you're done gawking, ask yourself, Just how much are these guys making?

Well… they're making a hell of a lot.

Consider this: from 2009 to 2015, the ten largest financial institutions in the US had to pay more than $179 billion—that's right, *$179 billion*—in legal settlements and penalties. Bank of America alone paid thirty-four different settlements totaling $77 billion.[8]

Now, think about that…

If they could afford to pay that much in *penalties*, how much money must they have made?

Don't ask me. I can't even imagine numbers like that.

But I know how they do it.

The returns Wall Street firms can generate off every dollar we give them are essentially infinite. Give them ten bucks, and they'll

---

8   Keefe, Bruyette & Woods, "Unshakable," chapter 5, LOC 1588 on Kindle.

repackage it, sell it, repackage it again, sell it again... and make a profit every time.

If they have one asset, they can sell it and create another product that leverages that asset. And then they have two assets. They repackage their assets over and over until they're making hundreds of billions of dollars off a single Hamilton—the one that you gave them.

They call this a fluid economic system, but really, it's a scheme for making investment bankers richer. It's essentially a scam—and it's built on our money.

We stake them because we're hooked. We can't break away from this sexy, adrenaline-and-testosterone-soaked soap opera called *Wall Street*.

* * *

There's a problem with all of this, though: we're making a bad bet, over and over again. And Wall Street knows it.

The late Jack Bogle, the founder of the Vanguard Group, spoke of this in 2016. He said something that blew my mind—and that's pretty hard to do because I've been in the industry for over twenty years.

"It's a highly profitable business," Bogle said in an interview published by Kiplinger.[9]

"The key of this whole thing is making sure investors get their fair share of the market's return. If you own an index fund, you can get the market's return for 0.05 percent. And if you have typical active management, the costs are at least 2 percent per year.

"So if the market returns 7 percent, the index investor gets 6.95 percent, and the active investor gets 5 percent. If you put 7 percent

9   Eleanor Laise, "Mutual Fund Legend John Bogle: What's Costing Investors Two-Thirds of Their Market Returns," *Kiplinger's Retirement Report*, published October 2016, https://www.kiplinger.com/article/retirement/T031-C000-S004-fund-legend-still-fighting-for-investors.html.

and 5 percent on a compound interest table, one dollar at 7 percent a year will grow over fifty years to about $30, and at 5 percent it will grow to about $10."

And then he said, "You're getting a third of the market return, even though you put up 100 percent of the capital and took 100 percent of the risk."

I couldn't believe it when I read it, but Bogle was right. He had nailed it.

Where else but Wall Street would anyone gamble like that? Nobody in his right mind would make that bet—but we do it all the time when we put our money in Wall Street.

We don't do it because we're idiots. We do it because we're misinformed.

Billy Walters, one of the most successful professional gamblers in the world, once said that the worst bet he ever made was putting his money into Wall Street. Now think about that: here's a guy with a net worth estimated at $100 million, a man who's made his living as a gambler, and he says Wall Street will suck you dry.

And why did Billy Walters, the world's greatest gambler, lose his bet? Because he was misinformed.

He had no idea what his actual risk was. He didn't have the data he needed to make a logical and mathematically sound bet because Wall Street kept that critical data hidden. And it still does. It's almost impossible to know the true cost of our investments because the numbers are buried in jargon.

In 2009 the Wall Street Journal reported the following:

The Government Accountability Office estimates that a one-percentage-point increase in 401(k) fees borne by plan participants would cut a worker's savings 17 percent over twenty years.

A 2007 GAO study found that many employees don't know how much they pay in fees, and that much of the fee information they get from their employers is "piecemeal." In turn, it found employers often don't get complete information from plan providers, and called for more oversight and disclosure of fees.[10]

So let's blow the lid off this. Here's what Wall Street doesn't want you to know:

If your money is in a tax-deferred account—an IRA, 401(k), or 403(b) plan—the expense ratio is around 1 percent on the whole. Transaction costs inside the fund amount to nearly 1.5 percent, and money coming in on a monthly or annual basis and money going out when people sell their shares means a cash drag on the account of another 0.83 percent.

Add that all up and your actual cost of being in a mutual fund is more than 3 percent a year. And your savings erode even more if you have a taxable account because you have to pay taxes on that amount too. The total costs of a taxable account are more than 4 percent a year.[11]

And these are the *good* funds. These are the fees for the all-revered Morningstar five-star-rated funds. If you're in the mood to pay even higher fees, there are lots of other funds out there to choose from.

---

10   Kelly K. Spors, "Small 401(k) Plans Often Pay Big Fees," *Wall Street Journal*, updated August 3, 2009, https://www.wsj.com/articles/SB100014240529702046 21904574251883387338254.

11   Ty A. Bernicke, "The Real Cost of Owning a Mutual Fund," *Forbes*, published April 4, 2011, https://www.forbes.com/2011/04/04/real-cost-mutual-fund-taxes-fees-retirement-bernicke.html#3a7572d63244.

* * *

That's what you unknowingly pay when you invest in the funds that the major brokerage firms—each one a stalwart of the investment universe—pitch to us.

They say, "Oh, don't worry about the fees. The operational costs are only 1 percent."

But they don't tell us that we're already paying 3 to 4 percent to start with.

And what does that mean to you? Well, over your lifetime, it could mean you're letting hundreds of thousands of your hard-earned dollars flow quietly to Wall Street.

This is death by a thousand cuts. It's like getting on a boat with a small leak that you don't even know is there—until you're out at sea and the water starts creeping up around your ankles. You're saving all this money for your retirement, and you're leaking dollars from the very moment you shove off.

* * *

Now let's be clear: Wall Street brokerages don't lie about these fees.

They don't have to. All they have to do is not talk about them.

They focus on their stellar performance or their high ratings, but they never talk about what we, the customers, are actually paying.

Maybe you think you're on top of all this, that you know how much a fund charges because you can go online and see what the operational costs are, and if the costs are less than 1 percent, you feel pretty good about yourself.

But that's just the tip of the iceberg.

The problem is that mutual funds and other Wall Street investment companies don't have to report the rest of their costs in plain, easy-to-understand English. They write their closure documents in the most convoluted language possible, and they bury those numbers—legally—in all the jargon.

If we want to know what we're really paying on a fund, we pretty much need to bring in a team of lawyers, CPAs, and financial experts to extrapolate the fees and interpret them. Only a select few fiduciary-based advisors are truly aware of what most of these investments cost. The others—the vast majority of financial professionals—don't have a clue. They're wearing blinders, and Wall Street loves it.

The mutual fund companies don't want us to know about the fees, so they have the brokers gloss over them. They say, "Look at how great these fund managers are… Look at how many years we've been in business… Look at how glossy this chart is… *Pay no attention to the man behind the curtain.*"

Well, it's time to pull back the curtain and let the sun shine in. Because the man standing behind it is selling us straight-up junk.

* * *

Fifteen years ago, back in 2004, Senator Peter Fitzgerald of Illinois said in a congressional hearing that the mutual fund industry was "the world's largest skimming operation… a trough from which fund managers, brokers, and other insiders are steadily siphoning off an excessive slice of the nation's household, college, and retirement savings."[12]

Fitzgerald led a group of lawmakers who tried to change the laws, but their bill never got past the Senate Banking Committee. And now, a decade and a half later, here we are—still stuck in a

---

12 Associated Press, "Fund Fees Denounced; Mutual Fund Whistleblower Tells of Beating," *New York Times*, published January 27, 2004, https://www.nytimes. com/2004/01/27/business/fund-fees-denounced-mutual-fund-whistleblower-tells-of-beating.html.

cycle of paying through the nose for junk from Wall Street, constantly being persuaded to move from one mutual fund to another.

The firm says, "Go with our fund group. We beat our Lipper peer group average. We're Morningstar five-star rated."

That sounds great, but what it doesn't say is that a vast majority of fund managers fail to get close to the benchmarks they promise. So we buy into a mutual fund, and it doesn't do as well as we expected, and what does our broker say?

"Oh, I can't believe it performed so poorly. But, hey, no problem. Let's switch to another mutual fund!"

And now we're on a hamster wheel, running ourselves to death, because our broker makes commissions off every mutual fund she sells us on. The industry, meanwhile, racks up front-end sales costs and continual internal fees…

And most of us don't even know it. We don't have a clue.

We don't know that we have options, that there are better investments out there with substantially lower costs. And why don't we know it? Because it's not in our broker's interest to show us anything beyond the Wall Street machine.

Maybe our best move is to pull $300,000 out of our portfolio to pay off the mortgage on our home. Maybe it's buying the house next door and renting it out or investing in a bed-and-breakfast or buying a fast-food franchise.

They're all options, and they're worth considering—but we won't hear them from our financial advisor because he needs to keep our money in the system.

There are so many other ways to make money, but we've been duped into thinking that Wall Street is not only the best way to produce wealth—it's the *only* way.

* * *

The sad fact is nobody actually gets rich off mutual funds. They may help enhance some wealthy people's long-term wealth, but I promise you those people acquired their wealth some other way.

If we don't have a pile of money already saved, a mutual fund won't get us one. But our broker won't tell us that.

Brokers sell mutual funds to us like they're miracle products. It slices! It dices! It will make you millions! You'll never have to worry again!

But it isn't, it doesn't, it won't, and we most assuredly *will* have to worry again.

Our biggest problems are budgeting, income generation, health concerns, and the timing of when we need money. There isn't a mutual fund on the planet that will solve those problems.

So whether you're pursuing perfect abs or a financially secure retirement, you need to have more than an Ab Cruncher 4700 Six-Pack or a mutual fund in your closet.

> If we don't have a pile of money already saved, a mutual fund won't get us one. But our broker won't tell us that.

You need to know exactly what you've got, who you are, and what you really want to accomplish. You need to devise a system that will work for you—only we're not wired for that. We've been trained to believe that the solution to all our problems is a product we can buy.

* * *

As a concept, mutual funds are great. But in practice, we're so misinformed about how they work that we don't know how to select them.

We're told that Fund A is different from Fund B, which is different from Fund C, but as far as our portfolios are concerned, they're all junk if they're not managed correctly. And the truth is 99 percent of us have no idea how to manage mutual funds correctly.

We're sold on the idea that they're all we need, but they're not.

A mutual fund is just one piece on a chessboard. If we're lucky, it's the queen—but even the queen needs a group of well-positioned knights and bishops and rooks and pawns to support it. We need to surround it with stocks and bonds and exchange-traded funds and annuities and real estate and precious metals. And most important of all, we need a chess master behind the board.

If you don't have a chess master who's studied the game and knows how to position all your pieces, you're going to be a mediocre player at best. And, sad to say, most brokers aren't chess masters. They just sell us stuff; they don't teach us how to use it to get the results we want.

* * *

When I meet with new clients, the first thing I do is try to get them to look past all the junk on their statement.

I don't care about what they have yet—I'm just trying to figure out who they are, where they want to go, and what they think they need.

What they have may be awesome, and I'll get around to analyzing all of it—but for the time being, they're not sitting in front of me because they need more junk.

They're there because they need to understand how their junk works and whether it's what they really need to hit their goals.

When I tell them this, it blows their minds because they've never had this conversation before. The only conversation they've had is about what product they should buy.

But I'm not interested in that. I want to be the architect who designs where they want to live for the rest of their life. I want to be the chess master they rely on to help them win.

Brokers focus on magical products. Buy this, buy that, and all our problems will be solved. Whatever we don't have, we need. Whatever we do have, there's something out there that's better or that will work great with it.

It's upselling, and brokers are great at it. If we have the Ab Cruncher 4700 Six-Pack, they'll say we also need protein shakes. If we have stocks, they'll tell us to add bonds. And maybe they're right. Maybe they could actually work for us, if we use them correctly.

But even if we do, they'll be back to sell us more stuff. And now we'll buy for sure because it worked the last time. We're hooked. We'll buy.

Have you ever walked into a car dealership and heard a salesperson say, "Your car is great. You don't need to buy a new one"?

Neither have I. What we always hear is "Check out the awesome features on the new model."

I'll bet you have a smartphone, and I'll double down that it's not your first. I'll bet you're on your third or fourth by now.

But why is that? Didn't your last one work just fine? Did you really need all those new features they upsold you on? Was the reception bad on the first one? Did it take crappy pictures? Was it intolerably slow?

Probably not. My guess is that you bought the new one because they told you it was so much better than the one you had. You didn't really need all those bells and whistles, but you were hooked, and you bought it.

Brokers do the same thing. They say, "Oh, you've got this mutual fund, but that one over there is so much better." And we keep buying, even if what we already have is serving us nicely.

That's why your broker isn't very upset when he sells you on a subpar mutual fund. If it doesn't work out, he'll just sell you another one. And if it's not much better than the last one, that's OK too. He'll sell you another. And another. And you'll keep on buying. All of us will because we're hooked on junk.

And here's the dark truth: we can't fix this. We're ripping ourselves off as a nation and depriving future generations of enjoying wealth and security because we're hooked on drugs, and detox is hard. But we'll never understand what it's like not to be hooked on junk until we get the toxins out of our system.

We need to rip off the Band-Aid and let the wound bleed for a while before it heals. But we won't do it because we hate the sight of blood.

How did this happen? How were we hoodwinked? How did we get so hooked? How did we let Wall Street grab all this power?

The answers are tied directly to the next storm we're going to talk about: the disappearance of pensions.

See the video on junk at
www.StormproofRetirement.com/junk

CHAPTER SIX

Storm No. 4

They Stole Our Future and Called It Freedom

I n 1978, Congress slipped a little gem into the Internal Revenue Code that was designed to give companies a new way to reward their executives and higher-paid employees.

From that point on, as an alternative to giving those employees taxable cash bonuses, the companies would be allowed to deposit money into savings accounts they set up for them—and the employees would pay no taxes on the money in those accounts until they retired and started making withdrawals.

The employees, who were mostly in high tax brackets, loved the idea—because let's face it, a sizable bonus isn't as big as it sounds when you have to fork over a large chunk of it to the IRS. They were well-paid, they didn't need their bonuses to pay the rent, and they were very happy to watch their money grow, tax-free, in a company-managed savings account.

The code change was a win-win for everyone, so nobody paid much attention to it for a couple of years—until a guy named Ted Benna put it under a microscope and looked closely at the fine print.

And what he saw hatched an idea that, in time, changed everything about how nearly all of us save for retirement today.

At the time, Benna was benefits manager and co-owner of a consulting firm in suburban Philadelphia—the cradle of American liberty. And what he conjured up was nothing short of a new Declaration of Independence, only this one wasn't from a despotic king.

This one was from the chains of pension plans, the retirement benefits most American companies had been providing to their workers for decades.

Benna looked at the tax code insertion—line 401(k)—and decided it didn't have to apply only to high-paid employees. The savings accounts could be expanded to include all workers, even the lowest-paid ones. As he himself explained,

I could use this section to design a plan allowing each employee to put into the plan whatever portion of the cash bonus he or she wanted.

The only catch was that I had to get the lower-paid two thirds to put enough money into the plan to allow the top one third to contribute as much as they wanted. Employees who put money into the plan would get a tax break but I knew this wouldn't be enough to get many of the lower-paid employees to put money into the plan.[13]

So Benna found a way to sweeten the pot.

This is when I thought of adding a matching employer contribution as an additional incentive. I was reasonably confident I could get

---

13   Ted Benna, "The Day I Designed the First 401(k) Savings Plan," Benna401k, 2008, http://benna401k.com/401k-history.html.

favorable results through the combined incentive of a tax break plus an employer matching contribution.[14]

And there it was—the inception of the modern 401(k) plan, the seed of our fourth storm.

Like a tiny tropical depression off the coast of North Africa that transforms into a Category 5 hurricane as it heads west across the Atlantic, this storm began very innocently. But four decades later, Congress's tiny insertion into the US tax code has become an albatross around millions of Americans' necks. We're going down with the ship.

> But four decades later, Congress's tiny insertion into the US tax code has become an albatross around millions of Americans' necks. We're going down with the ship.

* * *

For American companies, the 401(k) was love at first sight. For decades, they'd been funding and maintaining pension plans for their employees, a record-keeping and investment-management burden that had become an ordeal.

They wanted out, and now they had a road map.

They could inform their employees that they were halting all future contributions to their pension plans and that they would begin offering 401(k) plans instead. The existing pensions would remain intact—but no new contributions would be made, and new employees would not be allowed to participate.

It would take some time, but pensions would slowly fade away until they ceased to exist.

---

14   Benna, "First 401(K) Savings Plan."

* * *

If you're under the age of fifty, there's a good chance you've never seen a pension plan and that you don't have a clue how they worked. In essence, they were very simple.

Employees needed to know that when they retired, their final paycheck—the one they got on their final day—would not be the last one they'd ever see. So companies created giant investment funds to provide guaranteed, fixed incomes after retirement for everyone—from the CEO down to the maintenance crew—who had been working there for a specified number of years and was vested in the plan.

The companies and their employees, through paycheck deductions, contributed to the fund on a regular basis, and when an employee retired, he'd immediately begin receiving checks from the fund every month.

Exactly how much an employee got was determined by three factors: his age, how long he had worked for the company, and how much he was making when he left.

If an employee spent forty-five years at a company, she'd get more than the guy who worked twenty. If she spent fifteen years at three companies, she might get a monthly pension check from each one.

And here was the best part: she'd get them for the rest of her life. Whether she lived to be 70 or 85 or 103, that check would be directly deposited into her bank account, or it would arrive in her mailbox, every month after she retired.

Now, think about that for a minute. If you had worked for thirty years at Widgets Inc. and you retired from your job in 1970, you knew you'd be getting much more than a pat on the back, a gold watch, and a "We'll All Miss You Here at Widgets" greeting card when you punched the time clock for the very last time.

You'd also get security. You'd get a pension check the very next week instead of your paycheck.

And when it arrived, you knew you were going to be OK. Maybe you didn't have a personal savings account… maybe you didn't live in a home with a paid-off mortgage… but come hell or high water, that pension check and your Social Security check would go into your checking account every month. You'd have a steady income for the rest of your life.

And it wasn't just you. In all likelihood, your family members and friends were getting the same deal. Before the 401(k) arrived on the scene, 61 percent of Americans—more than three out of five—had some sort of a pension plan to support them when they retired.

* * *

Pension plans were great for employees. If you had one, you knew exactly how much money you'd be getting every month after you retired and that those checks would keep on coming as long as you were breathing.

But the plans weren't great for employers. They had to maintain them and do all the paperwork, and they had to keep sending out checks every month, without fail, to every worker who'd put money into the plan and had stayed on the job long enough to be vested in it—even if that worker hadn't set foot in the workplace for forty years.

The employers wanted an out, and suddenly they had one: Ted Benna's 401(k) invention. They could offer it to their workers, freeze contributions to their pension plan immediately, and someday, way out in the future, the day would come when some centenarian no one at the company remembered would cash his check and then check out himself.

And that would be the end of the pension plan.

* * *

Companies loved the concept, but it wasn't going to be easy to talk their workers into abandoning a popular plan that had been working successfully for decades. The employees were skittish and understandably so.

Not only were they being asked to contribute to a brand-new retirement scheme with a funny name but the more money they put into it, the less they'd be taking home in their pockets each week.

So the companies launched their big sell:

It's tax-free! *You contribute a percentage of your salary to this new fund, and you don't have to pay taxes on any of it! At least not until you retire!*

But even that wasn't enough, so they sweetened the pot.

We want you to do this so much, we're going to help you!

If you put 3 percent of your salary into the plan, we'll match that amount—and now you'll have 6 percent of your pay in there. That's twice the money *that you put in yourself!*

Once they said that, just about everybody wanted to get in on the game.

* * *

And then, just in case some workers still weren't sold on this new-fangled 401(k) thing, the heavy hitters from New York—the big boys on Wall Street—stepped in to seal the deal.

The financial houses were understandably ecstatic about the prospect of managing these new investment plans, and now that the door was open, they wanted much more than a foot in it. They were eager to offer hundreds or thousands of investment plans to 401(k) participants. The more, the merrier—because they'd be able to collect huge management fees on every one of them.

It would be a windfall for their shareholders, and all they had to do was sit back and reap the profits. On Wall Street, Ted Benna would be the goose who laid the golden egg.

The companies were still asking, "Why would our employees buy this? Why would they get rid of a stable income source?

"Even if they've paid off all their debts, they're still going to have to pay bills. They'll still have to eat. They'll still have to fill the car with gas. They'll have to pay their utility bills… They'll need money coming in, and a 401(k) won't guarantee they'll get it."

But Wall Street knew exactly how to frame the offer. The financial houses told big business not to worry, they'd handle the pitch. They'd tell workers the following:

Hey, why would you settle for a defined contribution plan with defined benefits? That was your father's pension plan. These are the eighties. What you want is… the American Dream*!*

But wait a minute. Wasn't the American Dream to "work hard, play hard, and live a prosperous life"?

No. That was your father's American Dream. These are the eighties. We have a new and better dream.

Going forward, the American Dream will be summed up in two words: get rich*!*

Wall Street redefined the dream, and here's how they sold it:

You work hard for your money. Why let your company invest it and tell you how much you can put in and how much you will take out when you retire?

We have an awesome new plan—it's called the 401(k)—and it lets you invest your money however you choose.

It has lots of great options. It has lots of great plans. And the best part is, it's all about… freedom!

Why would you want a pension plan that will pay you a stipend every month for the rest of your life after you retire when you can sign on to a new system that lets you decide how to invest your money for yourself?

Don't you want freedom?

Why would you want someone else to decide how to invest your money? Don't you want to be free *to make your own choices?*

With a 401(k), you'll be free *to make a fortune!*

And maybe you would. You *could* make a fortune—if you were a good fortune teller.

That was a big if, but it was a great sales pitch—and We the People bought it. We declared our independence, abandoned our safe and secure pension plans, and stepped up to the roulette wheel.

Because we love *freedom*!

* * *

The ship had sailed. The deal was done, and it was a win-win-win for everyone.

The companies loved the 401(k) because they could gradually eliminate their pension obligations. They looked at their new and supercool investment scheme and saw a way to tell their shareholders the following:

Great news! The way things are right now, we have no idea how long our employees are going to live, and we'll have to keep paying them until they die—even if they've moved to another country.

But we're going to sell our workers on a new program called a 401(k). It will do away with our pension obligations, and they'll buy into it because we're selling them freedom.

Wall Street loved it because the big financial houses would be home to all the investment schemes, the growth and money market funds that workers would put their deferred income into. Every last dollar they invested would be managed by Wall Street.

And finally, We the People loved it because we're Americans dammit, and we love *freedom*!

There was just one problem—the one thing nobody bothered to tell us, something that Kris Kristofferson and Janis Joplin almost said: *freedom's just another word for everything to lose.*

* * *

When we threw out our pension plans, we threw out our security too.

They duped us. Nobody told us we actually might not know everything we needed to know to choose our investments wisely. Nobody told us we could *lose* money.

Our employers wanted to get out of the pension business, so they encouraged us to listen to Wall Street.

Those guys have more money than Midas. You should listen to them.

Wall Street told us the following:

Aren't you kind of angry that the company you work for is using your money now just so it can give you a small income stream twenty or thirty years from now?

Wouldn't you rather take control of your own financial future? Don't you want to be free to make choices for yourself?

Don't you want freedom?

We nodded, and we said yes.

It was a good sell at the time. The stock market had two major bull runs in the eighties and early nineties, and workers were encouraged to think, "Yeah, how can they take all this money that essentially is owed to us? Why don't we use that ourselves? Why don't we invest our money in stocks and get rich just like our fat-cat bosses?"

Our employers and Wall Street said we could do exactly that if we just gave up the security of our pension plans and latched on to the freedom of 401(k) investments.

But here's what they didn't tell us.

They weren't really selling freedom. They were selling control.

They were telling us that no one knew better than we did about how to manage our money and that every single one of us should want to control every penny of it.

That's what they said, but there was something else that they didn't tell us. They knew that very few of us had the knowledge and education everyone needs to manage retirement money. That's an entire career unto itself.

> And we bought it. We sacrificed our safety net. We had a system in place that offered us security, and we gave it up to have the freedom to find, ummmm, security.

But they didn't care. They told us they wanted us to have financial security, and they were setting us free to find it ourselves.

And we bought it. We sacrificed our safety net. We had a system in place that offered us security, and we gave it up to have the freedom to find, ummmm, security.

They knew—and they didn't tell us—that this really was about control. We were like teenagers who want desperately to be treated like grown-ups… We wanted to control our lives even if it meant making some bad decisions. They saw that, and they gave us the freedom to do it—even if it meant screwing up our retirement years.

They gave us the control we craved, but they neglected to warn us that it's easy to climb into the cockpit of a jumbo jet and try to fly it across the country but we wouldn't do it because we know we'll perish in a ball of flames.

We were very willing to do that with our money, though.

They said, "You can be the captain. You can take off and land this plane." And we pulled back the joystick with both hands.

They knew—but they didn't tell us—that managing a retirement fund is like being a pilot. It's hard to fly a plane. Maybe you should take a few lessons and actually learn how to fly before you take off because there will be clouds and maybe a lot of turbulence up there.

But I'm not sure we would have listened even if they'd told us. We're a stubborn species. Once we heard the magic word *freedom!*, we wanted it, and that was all there was to it. They told us a 401(k) was the greatest thing since sliced bread, and we stepped behind the deli counter and made ourselves a sandwich.

We were greedy. We f***ed up. We listened to them. We couldn't see what was right in front of us: that they were very kindly offering to help us tear ourselves away from what was essentially a monthly paycheck we'd be getting for the rest of our lives.

They were stealing our security, and we let them do it.

That was the price of freedom.

* * *

Tell me, please… how do you define prosperity? What is freedom?

Is it a big ol' pile of money you can lose? Or is it knowing that no matter what happens you're all set up to get a steady stream of money that will never run dry?

I know what my grandfather would have said.

He had two pensions when he retired—one from the military and one from the State of Tennessee. He never made more than $34,000 a year when he was working, but by the time he died in 1999, he was taking in over $97,000 a year in retirement payments.

Think about that for a minute… Even if my grandfather hadn't saved a single dollar—even if he was nearly broke when he retired—he knew that a couple of deposits totaling more than $9,000 would show up in his bank account every month, without fail, for the rest of his life.

Now, if that isn't financial security, then I don't know what is. That's what pensions do, and that's what we essentially gave up forty years ago.

Remember when I said that 61 percent of Americans had a pension plan in the late 1970s? Today, it's down to 7 percent.

And the 93 percent of us who don't have a pension plan? We're standing at the craps table, hoping to roll a seven because Wall Street gave us all the freedom we wanted, but it didn't teach us how to use it.

There are people whose sole job is to help us manage our retirement money, but do you remember your company—or Wall Street—giving you any names?

Of course you don't. They didn't do that because Wall Street likes us dumb. It wants us to have no understanding whatsoever about how investment actually works because if we had a clue, we'd know how much the brokers are skimming off the top in fees and we'd try to nickel and dime them out of them.

They said if we invested in their 401(k) plan, we'd get a 7 or 8 percent return on our money—much more than any pension plan would pay us.

But they neglected to tell us that there were no guarantees. They didn't tell us that we'd be gambling and that sometimes you roll snake eyes and they clear the table.

Everything was great in the eighties and early nineties. We put the pedal to the metal and rode atop two of the greatest bull markets in history—but everything came to a screeching halt in 2008.

The Great Recession essentially erased all those gains, and if you had a 401(k) and had recently retired—or if you planned to retire soon—you saw your nest egg collapse right there in front of you.

Sorry, bub, but the yolk's on you. You'll have to go back to work now. And if your old job isn't available anymore, well, that's OK. Walmart needs greeters… except for one thing—I called Walmart, and they said they were full of greeters now.

* * *

Here's what Wall Street knew all along but never told you.

If you have a 401(k) and you're approaching retirement, you're riding a roller coaster—and that's exactly what you don't want to do in retirement. You've had enough freak-outs in your life. Now you want stability.

But you don't have stability with a 401(k). Even if you have a couple of million dollars invested in one right now, how do you know the market won't crash and wipe out half—or more—of it? Do you fully understand that you're gambling with your retirement money? What if your 401(k) suddenly turns into a 201(k)?

Wouldn't you be much more relaxed if you knew that your former employer was obligated to transfer $10,000 or so into your checking account every month, no matter what happens with the economy? Wouldn't it be nice, after all these years, not to worry about things you have no control over?

That is security. That is prosperity. That is *real* freedom.

When there's money coming in every month, guaranteed, you don't have to keep an eye on the Dow or NASDAQ or the S&P 500. You can sit back and read a good novel. You're finally free.

But nobody told you that because they didn't want you to know. Your company wanted out of the pension business, Wall Street wanted you in on its investment funds, and they conspired to suck you in—by selling you freedom.

But really, what they did was welcome you into the Retirement Casino. Have a seat at the blackjack table. You can make a ton of money if you're lucky, or you can lose a ton of money if you're not. Either way, it's on you. You can stand pat at sixteen or ask for a card. It's your 401(k), and you're in control.

But don't forget... You are fully liable for every dumb decision you make.

The casino doesn't care. It just wants you to come in and play. But never forget... The house always wins.

And Wall Street is the house. Maybe you'll have a great day or a great month or a great year... or maybe your investment funds will tank. Either way, the house will take its cut. Win or lose, a nice slice of your 401(k) goes to fees.

* * *

That was the plan all along. The real winners would be the shareholders, the fat cats in the executive suite. Wall Street knew that, and it let you think you'd be sitting at the table, playing with the big boys. But it also made certain not to tell you the rules of the game: sometimes you win, sometimes you lose—and you need to be able to afford to lose.

So... can you afford to lose?

You need to ask yourself that because it's the real issue here. They disguised what they were selling as freedom, but what they really sold us was control. And when it comes to our life savings—the money we accumulate over thirty, forty, fifty years at work—most of us lack the understanding and knowledge we need to do it right.

That's exactly what Wall Street wanted. The more ignorant we are, the more it can earn from our missteps.

The 401(k) experiment began when the oldest baby boomers were in their midthirties. And now, I'm afraid, it's going to end very badly.

Baby boomers undersaved like no generation before them. They have unparalleled credit and debt issues, and they don't have the guaranteed retirement income that their parents got from pensions. And that's too bad because they're going to need it. They'll live longer, and they'll have more health issues and higher costs to go with them.

That is where we are now, all thanks to the 401(k).

It has unraveled the fabric of our financial future, and even Ted Benna knows it.

When he thought up his great experiment, he had in mind something that would be no more difficult than a pension and every bit as safe.

But once Wall Street got involved, things changed dramatically.

"I would blow up the system and restart with something totally different," he said in an interview in 2011.[15] "Blowing up the existing structures is the only way we can simplify them."

---

15   Silvia Ascarelli, "The Man behind K-Cups Joins These 7 Inventors with Regrets," MarketWatch, published March 6, 2015, https://www.marketwatch.com/story/the-man-behind-k-cups-joins-these-7-inventors-with-regrets-2015-03-05?page=9.

But don't hold your breath. They stole our future and called it freedom, and they're not going to give it back without a fight.

See the video on freedom at

www.StormproofRetirement.com/freedom

CHAPTER SEVEN

Storm No. 5

A Tsunami of Emotions

O ur government is flat broke, we're buying crap on credit, they're selling us junk, they stole our future and called it freedom…

We're four storms in, but we're not done yet. There's one more to come, and it will combine with the others to form a perfect storm.

It's our emotions.

We are an emotional species. We gravitate to things that make us feel good, and we push away from things that make us feel bad. We experience joy and sadness. We seek pleasure. We run from pain. That's how we're wired.

Hundreds of thousands of years ago, our Stone Age ancestors developed a fight-or-flight response that still kicks in today when a crisis develops. That instinct to fight or flee came in very handy when our ancestors found themselves in the path of a charging rhinoceros, but it really isn't the best way to deal with the fluctuations of the stock market.

It kicks in anyway. When the stock market belly flops, despite the thousands of years we've spent learning to react to crises intelligently, we put logic on hold and react instinctively. Our fight-or-flight instinct takes over. As the cartoonist Walt Kelly famously said, we have met the enemy, and he is us.

Neuroscientists have determined that the parts of the brain that deal with financial loss are the same ones that are triggered in a life-or-death situation. And that's dangerous because financial loss requires a measured, well-considered response.

When we react to financial loss emotionally, we sabotage ourselves. But we do it anyway because what we feel is pain. And we'll do anything—even allow ourselves to become addicted to opioids—to avoid pain.

But sometimes it's good to embrace a different philosophy, one that says, "No pain, no gain."

If you're walking down a dark alley and a guy steps out of the shadows with a knife in his hand, your response should not be the same as when the stock market drops 600 points in a day. It shouldn't be, but it is. Whether the imminent disaster is physical or financial, it triggers the exact same receptors in our brains. That's just nuts—but it's a fact.

When someone says, "Don't worry, they're just paper losses," it flies in the face of everything that's been wired into our human fiber. Even if our concerns make no sense, there's something in us that's saying, "I don't know about that. I'm uncomfortable."

That guy saying it's fine, everything will be OK? What does he know? It's easy for him to say that—because he's not the one in pain. We're the ones who are suffering, and we'll do anything to stop the pain.

We'll do it fast. And we'll do it wrong.

We'll do the wrong thing at the wrong time, and we'll do it every time. We can't control it. It's how we're wired. It's who we are.

* * *

When I was in college, I was taught that the very first assumption of economics is that consumers behave rationally.

And now I want my money back—because if there's one thing I've learned in this business, it's that there's no such thing as a consumer who always behaves rationally.

If you're at a street fair and you come upon a booth that's got a few dozen people in front of it and they're all pushing to get to the front and they're clamoring, "Get me some of that! I want that. I need that…" Well, you know what happens next.

Whatever it is, you want one too. You weren't looking for it, and you don't really need it… but there's only a few left, and it costs only $19.95, and look at all those people reaching for their wallets. You don't want to miss out on this even if you're not sure what the thing is or what it does…

And then, sure enough, you buy it. Or maybe you buy two because whatever it is, it will certainly make for a great gift. Sure, it makes no sense whatsoever, but you do it anyway—because there is no such thing as a consumer who always behaves rationally.

Go to Walmart on Black Friday and see all the people snapping up eighty-four-inch flat-screen TVs. They probably have a perfectly fine seventy-eight-incher at home… but this one is eighty-four! And it responds to hand signals, and the price is right, and you just gotta have it.

And that's not all. While you're loading that eighty-four-inch TV into your cart, you see a twenty-speed blender in aisle seven that's going for only eighty-nine dollars—forty bucks less than it cost the day before. So what if you already have a fifteen-speed blender at home that works fine and will probably serve you well for another decade or two. This one has twenty speeds. It's five speeds better! So you grab the blender and put it in the cart with your TV.

Why? Because there's no such thing as a consumer who always behaves rationally.

> One of the very first assumptions of modern economic theory turns out to be wrong. We do **not** behave rationally. We only think we do.

So there you have it. One of the very first assumptions of modern economic theory turns out to be wrong. We do *not* behave rationally. We only think we do.

We'll drive ten miles from home to fill up with gas at a pump that charges two cents less per gallon than the one around the corner. Never mind that we'll waste a gallon of gas going there and back... never mind the routine wear and tear on our tires and brakes and everything else that can wear out and cost us hundreds of dollars... we're putting twenty gallons in, and that means we're saving... *forty cents*!

We can buy a pair of sneakers at a nearby mall. Or we can spend three or four hours taking two buses or an Uber—and two buses or an Uber back—to get them at a discount outlet where they cost seven dollars less. And we'll opt to go there because we're "saving" *seven bucks*!

Admit it: we do this. It's really dumb, but we do it. We're consumers, and we do not behave rationally.

* * *

We're even less rational when it comes to money. We set aside some of the money we earn every time we get paid, we put it into investment plans we hope will keep us comfortable when we retire, and we fool ourselves into thinking that we know what we're doing. And then we look at our statements and we can't help but think that no matter how well we're doing, we can do better.

We want to save even more, so we're always tinkering with our accounts. But we don't really understand what we're doing.

Since 1976, a company called Dalbar Inc. has been issuing its *Quantitative Analysis of Investor Behavior* (*QAIB*), a report designed to help industry professionals understand how investors behave and what they can learn from their behavior.

And here's what Dalbar has found.

Over the last thirty years, the overall stock market has seen an average gain of 10.16 percent—but individual investors, the ones who invest in the stock market, have seen an average gain of 3.71 percent.

In other words, if you put your money into the market thirty years ago and never looked at it again, you'd have gotten a little bit better than 10 percent on your money. But if you tinkered with it a lot, if you kept revisiting that money, looking for "better" ways to invest it, you'd have gone up 3.71 percent.

Now, think about that for a moment: You put up all the capital, you took all the risk—and you got only about 37 percent of what you would have gotten if you'd just put your money into a broad-based index.

And why did that happen? Because you told yourself, "Hey, I'm smart. I know what I'm doing. I can invest aggressively, and I can tolerate the ups and downs. No problem."

But you were wrong. You *did* have a problem because you were no different from the rest of us: you weren't wired to handle risk.

We're human beings, and we're terrible at handling risk. When the going gets tough, the tough get going—in the wrong direction. We suddenly forget everything we said about being aggressive investors. We tell ourselves, "Stupid! Why did I put my money into stuff that could go down this far this fast? How did I do that?"

Dalbar has found that we screw up as individual investors all the time because we can't handle the ups and downs of investment. Our brains aren't practical when things get emotional.

The *QAIB* cites "9 distinct behaviors that tend to plague investors based on their personal experiences and unique personalities":

- Expecting to find high returns with low risk

- Making decisions without considering all implications

- Taking undue risk in one area and avoiding rational risk in another

- Seeking to reduce risk but simply using different sources

- Copying the behavior of others even in the face of unfavorable outcomes

- Treating errors of commission more seriously than errors of omission

- Tendency to react to news without reasonable examination

- Belief that good things happen to me and bad things happen to others

- Relating to the familiar experiences, even when inappropriate

Let's look closely at three of these behaviors because they speak volumes about our emotions and how they're contributing to our perfect storm.

* * *

The first of the three is loss aversion. Our fear of losing money leads us to withdraw capital and always at the worst time. If stocks go down two days in a row, and the media pundits start yapping about bear markets and impending recessions, we lose our heads and let instinct take over. Our fight-or-flight instinct tells us to head for the hills, and we start dumping our money into "safe" investments that pay very low interest.

There's a term for this: panic selling.

The second behavior is narrow framing. We make decisions about a part of our portfolios without considering the effects our actions will have on everything else. We think, "Yikes, the market is tumbling. I need to put everything in my 401(k) into cash now!" But we fail to note that most of the rest of our portfolio is cash already. So if we sell our stocks and put everything into cash, we eliminate any chance of regaining our losses quickly if the downturn is temporary. If the slide suddenly reverses—if everything comes back quickly—we won't be part of it.

We do this all the time.

The third behavior is anchoring. We latch on to something familiar—an anchor—and then, no matter what happens, we adamantly refuse to cut the line and sail away. We say, "Well, my dad owned Ford stock, and it was always good to him, and it's been good to me, so I'm sticking with my Ford stock." Well, that didn't work out so well in 2008, when people said that about their General Motors stock. The company went bankrupt, and they lost everything.

My grandparents owned stock in the Winn-Dixie supermarket chain. They anchored themselves to it and watched $3.5 million turn into $200,000.

I remember people who said they'd stay with Enron forever. How'd that work out?

Anchoring means we're unwilling to accept change, that we're consciously choosing not to adapt. That's a very bad attitude for investment success, but we do it anyway.

Look, I get it. This is how we're wired. But "It's been really good to me" is one of the dumbest things I've ever heard in my line of work, and I've heard it hundreds of times. Whatever *it* is, I promise you… *it* doesn't know you from a hole in the wall, and *it* hasn't been good to you.

All this means is that you've been fortunate. You owned *it*— whatever it is—for a long time, and *it* came through for you. But have you become so anchored to *it* that you're not looking for something better?

If you were anchored to Microsoft, did you fail to notice Google? Were you so in love with Sears that you didn't notice Amazon?

We let our emotions rule our investment strategies, and that's a recipe for disaster. Only 20 percent of investment returns are based on the actual ups and downs of the market; the other 80 percent are based on psychology. And psychology is the thing most advisors are the least trained in.

Psychology? What are you talking about? I'm supposed to buy a five-star Morningstar fund that beats my Lipper peer group average, and I need to be diversified across small cap, mid cap, and large cap…

And you want to talk about psychology? What are you talking about? What's psychology got to do with all of this?

Well, believe it or not, psychology has pretty much everything to do with all of this. Investment pays into the pleasure-pain principle and our drive to achieve instant gratification. If we have a bad month, or if we have two bad months in a row, our brain asks, "Is this going to last forever?" And that causes us to reach out for a quick fix— which is exactly what we should not be doing.

We heat up at the exact time we should be staying cool. But we can't stay cool. We're not wired that way.

We see a small sand shark, and the next thing you know, we think we're surrounded by great whites and we're all going to die.

We leap before we look. We quickly decide that the company we're with isn't working, so we jump to another one that takes our entire portfolio and puts us into something that's almost exactly the same, except for the name. But that new name makes us feel good, so we make the switch and don't even think about all the fees we pay to do it.

Why? Because we're wired that way.

* * *

We have a very hard time understanding that we haven't been properly educated about investment strategy, so we inevitably let our emotions—not our brains—dictate what we do. And then we do the wrong thing at the wrong time, every time.

If we own some stock that goes up 25 percent in one year, we immediately start asking ourselves, "Should I pull out? Or should I let it ride?"

It's like having a ripe, juicy red tomato on the vine. If you pick it today, it will be great. But then you start thinking, if you pick it tomorrow, it could be greater. Or maybe it'll be perfect the day after that. Or maybe it won't. Maybe it'll start to rot.

Here's what isn't a maybe: you lack a statistical method for making this decision. You're just guessing, and your financial security is no place for guesswork.

> **It's been said that bulls and bears make money, but pigs get slaughtered. And it's true.**

It's been said that bulls and bears make money, but pigs get slaughtered. And it's true. If you're greedy, if you keep holding out for more, if you think whatever's good today is going to be great tomorrow, you're going to get slaughtered. You'll be bacon.

But you do that anyway because that's how you're wired. You're letting your emotions dictate your investment strategy—doing everything on a gut check and a hope and a prayer. And that's a horrible way to prepare for retirement.

There's a pleasure side to all of this too. The investment firms send us these beautiful, glossy brochures that tell us that if we invest $10,000 a year for just ten years and never put in another dollar again, we'll have millions when we retire.

That gets us to thinking, "Millions! I'll be rich!" And we rush to sign on to their offer because we're high on adrenaline and dopamine. It's the same feeling we get at the casino. Keep pumping quarters into that slot machine, and sooner or later we'll hit that multimillion-dollar jackpot.

We buy into the marketing literature, but we don't take the time to think through what we're doing. Maybe "millions" won't be a whole lot in twenty or thirty years. Maybe we'll invest $10,000 a year for ten years, and when the time comes to retire, we'll have enough saved up to buy little more than a couple of double-caramel soy macchiatos.

Those glossy brochures are selling us a concept. They're appealing to our feelings. They're telling us how great our lives can be, and they know we'll buy what they're selling because we're wired to seek instant gratification. We'll react emotionally, not intelligently, just about all the time.

* * *

Wealth is built over lifetimes, not overnight. Maybe you have the right plan for today, but what if it's the wrong plan for tomorrow? For next year? For forty years from now? If you have a good year, that's great. But maybe it's not unlike when you win your first hand at blackjack. You know what's going to happen if you stay too long.

Investment marketing is powerful. All those gorgeous photos of silver-haired couples walking along the beach, holding hands, playing with their beautiful grandkids. They're like what you see in beer commercials: young people, tanned and toned, with perfect smiles. Surf's up, let's head for the mountains.

Do you ever wonder why you don't see a lot of fat guys in beer commercials? It's because fat guys aren't living the dream. They probably drink the most beer, but the dream isn't a keg—it's a rippling, six-pack chest. It's a long-legged woman in a bikini lounging next to you on the beach with a lime wedge in her bottle.

That's the dream that sells beer to fat guys. And it's how the marketers sell investment opportunities to average folks. They sell the dream.

That's why we should always remember that even if we win that first hand at blackjack, the casino will be the ultimate winner if it can keep us at the table. The odds favor the house, and sooner or later, we'll cash in fewer chips than we had an hour or two ago.

That's why it's important to know, from the beginning, how much we're willing to play and how much we're willing to risk. If you're at the casino, you need to have a plan and stick to it, despite all the flashing lights and free drinks. And if you're building your life savings, you need to be able to tell the difference between what that glossy brochure is saying and what's real for you.

* * *

If you have almost all your life savings in a 401(k) or an IRA, and it's mostly market based, then you are literally gambling with your entire financial future. One hundred percent of it.

That's why investment houses keep sending us new brochures. They're saying, "Oh, you didn't like that last product you had? Well, check out this new one. This one is just right for you.

"What's that? You liked that old one? Well… look how much better this new one is."

They're constantly reinventing themselves because their top priority is to keep us from going elsewhere. When all is said and done, they're trying to sell us on something they know they'll be changing in three or four years.

In marriage, it's called the seven-year itch. But in investment, we're looking for a change after only three or four years. According to the Dalbar study, that's when investors start feeling that their investment strategies, no matter how good they've been, may not be as good as the twenty-five or so new ones that are out there and that there's a very good chance they're itching for a change.

That's why we, as individuals, underperform in our investments. We're antsy, and we're never satisfied. If things are going badly, we go looking for something good. If things are going well, we want something great. If things are going great, well… why can't they be greater?

We're human beings, and we crave emotional satisfaction. We're unwilling—and probably emotionally unable—to stick with what we've got for the long term. So we leap before we look, and inevitably we screw up.

* * *

We can't get rid of our emotions. The best we can do is be aware of them and try not to let them dictate what we do, to try to stop and look around and ask ourselves, Am I making this decision rationally or emotionally?

We cannot allow our emotions to stop us from asking, "What exactly am I doing here? I have my life savings in kind of an aggressive position, and maybe that's not such a good idea since I want to retire in six months. Should I maybe pull back a bit on my risk? I love the thrill of victory, but am I doing everything I can to avoid the agony of defeat?

"Or maybe I haven't really saved enough. Maybe I shouldn't retire yet. Maybe I should get a second opinion—an expert opinion—on all of this."

When the market goes up, everything is wonderful, and everybody is happy. But when it goes down, it's different for everyone. And sooner or later, the market *will* go down. I guarantee it. That's just how the market works.

But the problem, I've found, is that most people have no idea how a downturn of, say, 40 percent will affect them.

Will their 401(k) be down 38 percent or 62 percent? They don't know. They also don't know what they'll do when it does go down.

Maybe they'll stand pat and wait for it to come back. But if that's the plan, how long will they stick with it? Three years? Four?

They don't have a clue. All they know is that they hope the market doesn't go down.

Wall Street sold us on investing our future in the market, but they didn't educate us about how it works. They gave us all the tools, but they didn't tell us how to use them.

Why? Because it was in their best interest not to.

All those tools they gave us are useless if you don't understand what they do and if you don't understand your limitations. You can hand me all the tools in the world, but they won't make me a carpenter. If I want beautiful wainscoting in my home, I know for sure that I'm my very last choice to design, build, and install it. If I want it done right, I'll call in someone who knows what to do with all those wonderful tools I've been given.

So why don't we do that when it comes to investing our life savings? We get our hands on the tools, and all of a sudden we think we're qualified to make life-determining investment decisions for ourselves and our loved ones. But we're so overloaded with information, we can't begin to analyze all our options and make reasoned decisions.

So we rely on our emotions instead. We say, "I don't have time to read these thousands of pages. I'm just going to go with the one that feels good."

Well, it may feel good, but it may be entirely wrong for our situation. Or maybe we pick something that's far too aggressive for our situation, and we don't fully understand that.

* * *

Our emotions lead us to seek the highest return, which is great when things are good. We see funds that are showing annual returns of 9 percent, and we put all our money into them.

And of course, we steer clear of the bonds and stable value funds that are doing only 1 to 3 percent because who wants low returns?

Well, that's great in a bull market. But just wait till things turn bearish and that 9 percent turns to minus 9 percent. I promise you when that happens, you'll wish you'd picked some bonds. Those are the safe investments that protect us from disaster when everything goes downhill.

Daniel Kahneman, who won the Nobel Prize for his studies in behavioral economics and on the psychology of judgment and decision-making, said that familiarity is not easily distinguished from the truth and that frequent repetition is a reliable way to make people believe in falsehoods.

And what have all those discount trading platforms been telling us? We can do it on our own. They'll give us all the tools, and we can control our destinies.

Why don't they just say they're going to give us more information than we can imagine but they're not going to tell us how to use it because they really don't care?

What don't they just say that they're here to help us lose our money, that if we're going to lose it, we might as well do it with them?

And why do we fall for this?

That last one's easy. It's because we're ruled by our emotions, and our emotions tell us that we're good enough and smart enough to succeed at this very complicated game.

And maybe we are. Maybe we'll do well for a while. But what will we do when something goes wrong and our palms get sweaty?

What will we do when the market tumbles and it feels like a rhinoceros is coming full speed in our direction? What will we—what will *you*—do when fear takes over?

All we can do is understand that sooner or later, we will fail, so we need to be prepared. We need to build a system that accepts failure but is designed to prevent catastrophic failure.

If we've put ourselves in the cockpit, are we prepared to deal with severe turbulence? Will we deal with it calmly and rationally, or will we respond to it emotionally?

We're controlling the plane, so this is no time to start randomly pushing every button on the console, hoping something works.

This is our life savings. We don't want to panic and sell off everything when a downturn comes.

* * *

Never forget this very basic fact: money is emotional. If you're controlling your money, you can't separate it from your emotions.

If you think you can, you will fail. And if everyone is failing, you'll fail the fastest.

All of us will have some form of failure in our portfolios or financial lives, and all we can do is make sure that when it comes, it isn't catastrophic. That when we're in the cockpit and one gauge fails, it doesn't knock out all the others.

If you think you're able to do all of this yourself, then I have just one final question.

Are you sure?

---

www.StormproofRetirement.com/emotion

CHAPTER EIGHT

The Retirement Solution

I f you're a doctor, you must provide the best treatment you can for your patient. It's the law.

If you're a lawyer, you must provide the best representation you can for your client. It's the law.

But if you're a financial advisor or a broker, there is nothing that says you must provide the best advice to the people whose money you manage. There's no law to prevent you from doing what's best for you.

That's boneheaded, of course, but it's true. The financial services industry has no law that requires its practitioners to do what's best for their clients. Offering great advice is optional.

But why wouldn't your advisor give you great advice? Why wouldn't he do everything he can to make sure you get the best return on your investments?

It's because your best interests may conflict with his.

When a financial advisor or broker puts your money into an investment plan, he gets a commission. When he moves your money from one plan to another, he gets a commission. When he tells you your investment in Coke is stagnant, so let's move everything to Pepsi, he gets a commission.

No matter what, he gets a commission.

Now, if he has to choose between recommending a good investment that will pay him a large commission and a great investment that will pay him a smaller one...

Which one do you think he'll choose?

OK... reality check here. Not all advisors are commission mongers. And just because they want to earn a living doesn't make them bad people. Some may even choose not to charge commissions on selling us investments... but the point is that they could—and we would never really know the difference.

There are more than 310,000 financial professionals in the US, and 98 percent of them are free to encourage you to invest your money in opportunities that may or may not be right for you—but will pay them investment commissions no matter what.

If your investment does great, your advisor gets a commission. If it goes toes up and leaves you with nothing, he gets a commission. You're gambling, and he's cashing winning tickets.

* * *

This is no way to plan for retirement, and it's why you should be skeptical about working with a financial advisor or broker whose best interests may clash with yours.

Fortunately, there is an alternative: a fiduciary, a fee-only advisor who always puts you first—because he has no choice in the matter.

He can't take a commission or any other incentive for putting you into a securities product. It's against the law.

You pay a fiduciary a set fee, and that's all he gets. And what you get in exchange is an advisor whose one and only obligation is to do what's best for you.

That means your fiduciary will be working on much more than your investment portfolio. He'll be monitoring not only your investment allocation but where your return is going. And he'll be seeking answers to a lot of questions that a commission-based financial advisor won't bother to ask, including the following:

- How much of your investment income is being siphoned off for taxes?

- Should you consider yanking your money out of the market and buying passive real estate?

- Should you start collecting Social Security now, or should you wait?

- Is it better to take your pension in a lump sum, or should you wait until the company starts paying you monthly?

- What about long-term care? Should you consider it? Is it worth the cost?

- What about your estate plan? Nobody in the history of human existence has ever failed to die, so it's pretty likely that your turn will come around someday. Assuming it does, what do you want to have happen to any money that's left in your account? Do you want it to go to your spouse and your kids? Would you like to give it all to charity? Do you mind if it goes to Uncle Sam?

A retirement plan is a huge puzzle with lots of pieces, and these are just a handful of them. But most people pay a lot of money to financial advisors or brokers who handle only one piece. Fee-only fiduciary advisors, on the other hand, are in the business of helping their clients solve the whole puzzle.

They have to. They're required by law to guide you through all the whirlwind crap and do what's in your best interests, not the investment firms'. Because they get no securities commissions, their only interest is you.

But here's something most people don't realize, and that you need to keep in mind.

Of the more than three hundred thousand financial advisors out there, less than 10 percent can say they're fiduciaries—but 80 percent of that 10 percent are dually registered, which means they can say that they're working both as fiduciaries *and* for a brokerage house.

They can wear a hat one day that says they're acting in your best interests, and then they can switch hats the very next day and sell you an investment product that pays them a commission.

You want the guy who wears only one hat—the one with your name on it. That's a fiduciary-only advisor. You pay him a fee, and he works for you.

* * *

Now maybe you're thinking, "Why should I pay my hard-earned money to someone who will manage my retirement plan? I'm good with money. I'm smart. I got As in math. I can do it all myself."

Well, OK, you're right. You *can* do it yourself, no doubt about it.

But now ask yourself this.

Why do LeBron James, Tiger Woods, Mike Trout, Tom Brady, and Serena Williams have coaches? They're the cream of the crop, the best in the world at what they do. Why would they need help from anyone?

Here's why: because even they can't focus on everything. They keep their coaches close by to spot the things they can't see—a hitch in the backswing, a change in grip, their release point, their launch angle.

Or maybe nothing's wrong at all. Maybe they're doing great. When everything's clicking, why do they still need that coach in their corner?

Because that coach will help them control their temperament and keep focusing on winning, which is the whole point of the game.

That's how you should think about your investment portfolio. Sure, you can manage it on your own—but can you be great at it without some expert coaching?

This is your retirement. You've worked your entire adult life for this. Don't you want it to be great?

Do you really want to steer this ship yourself… or do you think it might make sense to put an experienced captain at the helm, someone who knows how to navigate through rough seas while you sit back in your longue chair and enjoy the ride?

I suspect you already know the answer to that. But if you still don't, then try adding this to your equation.

Vanguard (yes, the same Vanguard Investments that revolutionized the world of low-cost investing) published an article[16] a while back that showed that a skilled fiduciary-only advisor, over time, can add over 4 percent annually to our portfolio returns. Now that is a lot of value over time!

Let's take a deeper look to see how Vanguard calculated this value.

---

16 Francis M. Kinniry Jr. et al., *Putting a Value on Your Value: Quantifying Vanguard Advisor's Alpha*, Vanguard Research, September 2016, https://www.vanguard.com/pdf/ISGQVAA.pdf.

VANGUARD ADVISOR ADDED VALUE	
Low-cost models	0.40%
Rebalancing	0.35%
Behavioral Coaching	1.50%
Asset allocation	Up to 0.75%
Withdrawal Strategy	Up to 1.10%
TOTAL FIDUCIARY ADVISOR VALUE	**Up to 4.10% annually**

That's why you shouldn't do this yourself. You should be looking for a fiduciary to help you because it's more than just your retirement. It's your loved ones' future.

* * *

Once you've brought a good fiduciary on board, she'll have her work cut out for her. She'll have to devise a personal set of solutions to multiple issues that may complicate your portfolio:

- the tax trap,

- inflation,

- being pensionless,

- market risk, and

- emotions.

For decades, we all were told that we should set aside a slice of our income and put it into an investment plan that allowed us to defer paying taxes until we retired.

But now we're starting to understand that maybe that wasn't the best advice. Most of us who did what we were told now have entirely too much of our wealth sitting in tax-deferred accounts—and it's going to cost us down the road.

So your fiduciary's first job will be to help you shift your assets to avoid the tax trap. Here's what she should tell you.

Think of your assets as being divided among three buckets of money: taxable, tax deferred, and tax-free.

In a perfect world, you should have no more than six months' worth of living expenses in the taxable bucket because paying taxes annually on your money really eats away at your returns!

The rest should be in your tax-deferred and tax-free buckets—but this is where things get complicated.

How much you put into your tax-deferred bucket depends on your circumstances, but if you can keep the amount within an appropriate range,[17] your fiduciary may be able to help you withdraw all of it without paying any federal taxes. Think about that for a second… You'll have put the money into tax-deferred accounts, but you'll be taking every dollar out of them potentially tax-free—if your plan is structured correctly!

Do this right, and you're already saving more money than you're paying your fiduciary. It's a winning hand for both of you.

But most people don't know how to do this. They've put entirely too much money into their tax-deferred bucket, which means they'll have to pay taxes on their Social Security benefits.

---

17 Current tax laws establish the range for less than $680,000 to be in tax-deferred savings to potentially eliminate taxes on Social Security.

And if you're one of them, well… do you really want to do that? After working for decades to maximize your Social Security benefit, do you really want to give some of what the government is finally paying you right back to it because you didn't plan well?

Keep in mind that we're not talking about just a couple of bucks here. The average couple that avoids paying taxes on Social Security benefits will save more than $9,000 a year for the rest of their lives. Over twenty-five years, that's more than $200,000 in federal tax savings alone!

And what about the third bucket, the tax-free one?

You've got six months' worth of living expenses in the first bucket and less than $680,000 in the second bucket. The third bucket gets everything that's left. It can be a Roth IRA, or use Roth conversions, or a Roth 401(k) or some properly structured insurance…

But whatever it is, no matter how you structure it, everything else you have saved for retirement should all go here into the tax-free bucket.

Got all that? Maybe you do, maybe you don't, but I think this is a good time to repeat the question I asked earlier: Do you think you can do this on your own? Do you know everything you need to know about shifting your assets to avoid paying taxes once you've retired?

I'm willing to bet that you don't. But I know you can still do this—with some help from a skilled fiduciary who understands not only the investment world but the taxation world too.

* * *

The next item on your fiduciary's to-do list will be solving for inflation, which is the silent killer of all wealth.

Let's say you've decided that you'll be comfortable making $75,000 a year when you retire and that you plan to quit working when you reach sixty.

Well, hooray. That does sound pretty good.

The problem is… by the time you hit eighty, with a very moderate inflation rate of 3 percent, you'll need $152,000 a year to buy what $75,000 cost you when you turned sixty.

And if your reaction to that is "Yikes!" then consider this.

If the inflation rate goes to 4 percent, you'll need to bring in more than $200,000 a year when you turn eighty just to maintain the $75,000-a-year lifestyle you had planned.

But, you ask, won't cost-of-living increases in Social Security payments make up the difference?

You can't be serious.

Sadly, if you look at the front page of a recent Social Security statement, the government has already warned you in black ink. It states: "Without changes, in 2033 the Social Security Trust Fund will be able to pay only about 75 cents for each dollar of scheduled benefits."

So instead of Social Security helping us with our inflation concerns, there's a good chance they'll be giving us even less in the future.

The only thing that will make up the difference will be a broadly diversified portfolio of investments and income sources that not only grow over time but increase their payments to you too.

That portfolio has to be consistent because if you have even one bad year out of five, the numbers won't work out. But it's doable. There are dozens of ways to get this right if you—or someone in your corner—knows how to do it.

You can do it if you have access to a pension that has an inflation adjustment, or if you can set up a personal pension that pays an annuity with inflation adjustments. You can do it if you can adjust the money you have in the market in a way that maximizes your return during a downturn. You can do it by investing in real estate, which offers rent income that you can typically increase every three or four years.

You can do it by investing in market-linked CDs—FDIC-insured, guaranteed certificates of deposit that are linked to the stock market. If the market goes up, so does your value. If the market goes down, your investment is FDIC insured. This is one of the safest ways to potentially solve for inflation without risking any extra principal.

But you have to know how to do it.

* * *

The next piece of the puzzle your fiduciary will tackle is what to do if you are among the 78 percent of Americans who are pensionless and need to develop a steady stream of income.

You can't retire without an income stream—Social Security benefits just won't cut it. Pension payments traditionally provided that additional steady income, but pensions are becoming rarer every day. If you have one, great. But the odds are you don't.

So how do you create a steady stream of income?

There are lots of ways to do it. The most important thing is that you have to do it *right*.

You can't look at your assets and think, "Hey, I've got a big pile of money. Everything is great" because that pile needs to keep growing to offset inflation, and it can't do that if it's just sitting there. Somehow, that big pile of cash has to find a way to get bigger over time.

You can do it through stock dividends. You can do it by renting out a vacation condo on Airbnb. You can do it through insurance. You can do it any number of ways, but you have to do it—because you need a steady stream of income and most of us don't have a pension to provide it.

And you need multiple sources to provide that income stream because stuff happens. Companies can cut dividends. Municipalities can change their zoning regulations. You never put all your eggs in one basket.

You need a multifaceted plan that has, at minimum, three different sources to feed your income stream. What they are is up to you... Do you want it to adjust for inflation? Does that not matter because you have other components that do?

Everyone's situation is different, and you'll do what's best for you. But you'll absolutely have to do something.

If you can do it on your own... great! Just be sure to get it right.

But if you can't, that's not a problem. Your fiduciary can.

* * *

The next item on your fiduciary's list is solving for market risk.

The biggest fallacy we've all been taught is that the stock market always comes back.

That's technically true, but it's very misleading. The market always comes back, but your money doesn't always come back with it. When we're closing in on retirement, or when we're already in retirement, we have to protect our downside.

This is not a choice. Ignore this at your own peril. Let's do some simple math.

> **The biggest fallacy we've all been taught is that the stock market always comes back.**

If the stock market goes down 50 percent and then comes back 50 percent... you're not back where you started.

If it starts at, say, 10,000, and it goes down 50 percent to 5,000, and then it comes back 50 percent, it's all the way back to... 7,500. Do that in dollar bills, and you've gone from $10,000 to $5,000 to $7,500.

To get back to where it was before it lost 50 percent, the market needs to come back 100 percent. Sooner or later, of course, it'll do just that. It'll come back 100 percent and keep on growing because it always has.

But when you're sixty-five or seventy or eighty years old and you've overinvested your assets in the stock market, will you be in a position to sit back in your rocking chair and wait for it to do that?

When you were young and working, you were able to put your money into a 401(k) plan, hopefully with some matching investment from your employer. You bought low, and you had the luxury of time on your hands. You could sit back for a couple of decades and watch the market zigzag inexorably higher.

But when you're approaching retirement—or once you're in it— everything changes because you lose the company match and you no longer have time on your side. Taking money out to live on reduces your potential to earn compound interest, and if there's a downturn, you may not have time to ride it out. This is why so many investors worry about running out of money.

Now, don't get me wrong. I'm not advocating pulling everything you have out of the stock market. I'm just saying that the risk strategies we employed when we were younger need to be adjusted. We need to find ways to get an attractive rate of return with substantially less risk than we felt comfortable accepting when we had time on our side.

There are numerous strategies for this. They don't start with calculating how much return you'll get. They start with knowing how much standard deviation you'll have in your overall investment portfolio.

Most financial professionals don't teach you this. They don't get it—because they're not trained to get it. They're trained to sell, not to understand how to solve for our biggest fear... having enough money for the long road ahead.

The ones who get it are institutions and endowments. They understand that they have to sustain themselves over long periods of time, even though they know they'll be spending some of their wealth on an annual basis.

And that's what you'll have to do in retirement. You'll have to be pouring some money out of your bucket to sustain yourself, and you'll have to keep increasing what's in that bucket while you do it.

Institutions and endowments do this by covering their downside to generate a market-type return without risk, and you can do it too. It's not easy, but you can.

It's not about the ups; it's about the downs. It's about understanding the standard deviation of your current portfolio, which is something you need to do immediately and in depth.

Once again, of course, you *can* do it yourself. But you'd better get it right because you can't afford not to. Market risk is going to be the number one reason people run out of money in the next decade.

And don't just take my word for it. The Center for Retirement Research at Boston College, which the *New York Times* called "the nation's leading center on retirement studies," says that if the stock market has one more major downturn, there's no way the vast number of baby boomers will be able to recover.[18]

This is a solvable problem, but you have to know your standard deviation before you find the solution that's right for you.

---

18 Barry P. Bosworth, *Impact of the Financial Crisis on Long-Term Growth*, Center for Retirement Research, June 2015, https://crr.bc.edu/wp-content/uploads/2015/06/wp_2015-8.pdf.

It might be FDIC-insured, market-linked CDs. They have zero risk, so you can completely control your downside, and they might give you a 6–7 percent return in a good year. That's nowhere close to what you'll get if the market goes up 50 percent. But if the market goes down 50 percent, the worst it can give you is no return—zero loss, which is a helluva lot better than the hit you'll take from the market.

Zero risk can be very attractive when you're seventy years old.

If you can earn 4 or 5 percent with zero risk, is that better or worse than the 6 or 7 percent you might earn with risk still on the table? There's no right answer to this. It's a personal choice that you'll make based on how much you have and how much you're willing to risk.

It's a hard choice. You can make it by yourself, if you want. But maybe you could use some help from someone who can look at things objectively because he won't be affected personally.

* * *

This brings us to your fiduciary's final challenge: helping you solve for emotions.

Maybe you've got what it takes to figure everything out for yourself. Maybe you can solve your tax trap, anticipate inflation, adjust to being pensionless, and plan for market risk.

That's awesome! If you can do all that, we have just one final question: How will you behave under pressure? What do you think you'll do when the you-know-what hits the fan?

I grew up in Kentucky, so I'm genetically inclined to be a college basketball fan. Every year, when a new group of unbelievably talented young men walk onto the hardwood to play for the University of Kentucky, I sit back and marvel at their ability.

But I've also learned that when the game begins, their talent isn't all that matters. There are a few dozen teams with incredibly talented players. What separates the greatest from the merely great is how they react under fire.

When the shot clock is dwindling down and there's a kid out there just a few months out of high school and he's playing against people who are substantially more experienced than he is… he has to know that their job is to make him fail.

And now the game is tied, the ball is in his hands, and he has to sink a three before the buzzer sounds.

That's how it is in retirement. Are you ready for it?

You may have done everything you can to protect yourself when *something* goes wrong—but what will you do if *everything* goes wrong, *all at the same time?*

It doesn't have to be a market-related incident. Different things happen to everyone. Some people will have health-related issues. For others, it'll be a family emergency. Still others may have to relocate. Some may lose good jobs—and the pensions they were counting on—two years before they planned to retire. Or maybe they'll keep their job, but the company will change the pension structure two years before they plan to retire.

> You may have done everything you can to protect yourself when **something** goes wrong—but what will you do if **everything** goes wrong, **all at the same time?**

How will any of us react in situations like these? Will we be able to keep our emotions in check so we can do what's right not just for now but also for the future?

This—our emotional state in a crisis—is the biggest reason why most investors should have a skilled, fee-based, fiduciary advisor in their corner.

Your fiduciary will be there to help you get through all of this. He won't sugarcoat it. He'll be honest and tell you that, yes, this is a crisis, and it really sucks. But then he'll tell you to go home, get some sleep, and come back tomorrow, when he and you, together, will figure out what to do next.

It won't be fun, but you'll put your heads together and get through this. You'll hammer out a solution and get back on track.

Your fiduciary will help you in this way because it's what he does. He knows what works, and he's not going to let you do something stupid just because your emotions are keeping you from seeing clearly. This is why you brought him on board.

More often than not, you solve emotion by pulling it out of the equation—and the only way you can do that is to have someone else do it for you. You can gripe about performance, you can gripe about fees, you can gripe about all sorts of things—but you need this guy. He's there to make sure you check your emotions at the door, see things clearly, and do what's right.

In 2016 Vanguard studied the value that quality fiduciaries bring to their clients, and it determined that it's over 4 percent a year if they do things correctly.

Now consider this... A fiduciary will typically charge you 1.5 percent or less of your portfolio every year. Whether you know it or not, you're probably paying 3 percent to your mutual fund managers and your financial advisor, and you're reaping 4 percent less in value. So your fiduciary is essentially providing an outcome that's more than 5 percent higher.

Vanguard says 1.5 percent of that is gained simply by controlling client emotions. If you have a $1 million portfolio, that means a fiduciary is adding $15,000 to it every year just by not allowing you to be an idiot.

That's what happens when we have someone at the helm who can separate our emotions from our decisions. We simply have to face the fact that we're not wired to do it alone. None of us are. We can't always fix all our problems by ourselves. In a crisis situation, we all want an objective person who can see things clearly.

That's your fiduciary.

---

www.StormproofRetirement.com/radio

Your Voyage to Retirement

I always keep in mind a couple of eloquent maxims my grandmother passed on to me when I was young:

"Honey, it's never the wrong time to do the right thing."

And "Honey, you can't do better if you don't know better—and now that you know better, what are you going to do?"

All of us should keep those words of wisdom in mind as we test our seamanship and steering in a perfect storm. Experienced fiduciaries are like the best dinghy sailors. They're often very good at heavy air steering because they can see "survival" weather more often that most of the "cruisers"—the advisors who do not subscribe to the fiduciary standard of advising.

Storms rarely arrive unannounced. Experienced fee-only advisors can see them approaching because they've been out in them before. With proper forecasting, you too can run for the shore or venture into open sea to experience the beauty it has to offer. A skilled fiduciary will help you with decisions and stay by your side to help you maneuver the calm and stormy seas.

If you've already retired, or if you plan to retire in the next five years, you know we're in the crosshairs of a perfect storm. We can't avoid it. The only question now is, How well have we prepared for it, and do we understand the choices we can make once we're in it?

Will we lie ahull—just sit out there with our sails down and wait for it to pass? We've heard this concept before. Our advisor told us to ride out the market, that it would come back, that we were in this for the long haul.

And how did you feel about that?

Advisors often offer this advice because they simply aren't skilled enough to help their clients in crashing waves. A skilled advisor, on the other hand, will keep you in control of your boat's angle to the waves and help you avoid the rolling motion that can feel so debilitating.

I've spoken with countless people about this, and I've found that most of them want to take a break, relax, and not worry about suffering a huge market loss and losing much of their life savings.

Imagine a break from the relentless pitching and pounding of market woes… a chance to go on vacation… to donate more to your church… to help out a charity… or heck, to go buy a bigger boat. The lost art of heaving allows you to "park" in open water and enjoy its luster.

The same is true by fiduciary standards. Skilled fee-only advisors have models to navigate and/or allow you to *heave to*—not actually to stop but to achieve a motion that is dramatically more stable and pleasant than lying ahull and missing out on other potential investment opportunities.

Safe money certainly doesn't mean you have to hide it under a mattress and do nothing. There are other ways to keep making leeway in a storm.

* * *

In a recent poll, 65 percent of respondents distrusted the financial services industry to act in their clients' best interests.[19] Could it be that those investors are still angry about what they were led to believe and where they were headed before the crash of 2008? Are the same messages being remarketed to us again today? Are we falling back into old habits?

> Safe money certainly doesn't mean you have to hide it under a mattress and do nothing. There are other ways to keep making leeway in a storm.

Everyone remembers the tragedy that struck us and how we weathered through the long, wet, cold market times for the years that followed. But eventually, we forget how we felt. We lose our fear of markets, and we return to our behaviors of investing and being marketed to.

We lose our fear of market risk too. Do you recall how you felt when the market tanked? Are you risking another big loss in another storm, or are you in position to carry on even in a perfect storm?

* * *

What most investors don't know is that they have a choice. If conditions are wrong or if they worsen, and if they've chosen a fee-only fiduciary instead of a commission-based consultant, they'll be abso-

---

19   Paul Dietrich, "Almost Two-Thirds of Clients Don't Trust Advisors to Act in Their Best Interest: Poll," accessed Nov. 14, 2019, https://advisorhub.com/resources/almost-two-thirds-of-clients-dont-trust-advisors-to-act-in-their-best-interest-poll/.

lutely certain that their anchor or mooring lines are secure—because that's the most critical part of a fiduciary's job description.

Fiduciaries do better when all of us do better. It's that simple. They say the most dangerous ship in the ocean is an empty one because the weight of cargo helps stabilize a ship against the waves. That's true for investors as well when they share their weight with a fiduciary on board to help keep them afloat.

A fiduciary is obligated to act in our best interest in all aspects of our finances.

It might be a tax plan that stays current with tax legislation so we don't end up paying hefty fees or taxes out of our investment portfolio.

It might be an income planning strategy, a bucketed strategy your fiduciary uses to manage your money along time horizons. It allows money to be balanced, and it ensures liquidity for our needs while still allowing money to grow in long-term investment options.

It might include a long-term care plan or getting rid of a long-term care plan and replacing it with something that doesn't cost as much.

It might include estate planning to help you pay substantially less in taxes, fees, and court costs. For skilled fiduciaries, it's not just investment management; it is life management.

It's safe to say that a sailboat in a storm is only as good as its sails. When you consider the challenge of capturing the force of the wind and propelling your boat in a huge storm, it's only natural to consider the differences between various sails and how they work.

The same is true of our investments. We should understand how they work and how our portfolio is built. A fiduciary will spell out our plan in plain English and give it to us in writing. And if we've selected a quality fiduciary, we'll know for sure that the plan is right for us because a good fiduciary won't engage us as a client if he can't add value to our situation. Fiduciaries just don't do that. It's not how they think.

* * *

Ships don't always head for the nearest port when a storm is approaching because not all ports offer the same kind of shelter.

The same is true of financial advisors.

Most of us think our financial advisor's job is to manage our portfolio and help us answer questions about how to plan for our retirement.

But that isn't really what we should be looking for. What we really need is a skilled person who can help us understand exactly where we are today and what we need to do going forward.

This is a personalized strategy, one that is unique to each of us. It's just like steering a ship in a storm. Because not all ports offer the same protection, a captain may look for a harbor near high mountains or cliffs that can protect it from the winds.

In a perfect storm, a good captain would steer his ship to an area of the ocean that will see the shallowest waves and lowest winds. That's usually the side that's counterclockwise from the storm's leading edge.

A good fiduciary is obligated to do the same.

It can be hard to predict how severe a storm will be just by looking at it. Sometimes, there are ominous skies that suggest the apocalypse is coming—and then practically nothing happens. At other times, it may not look too bad—and then it turns out to be the end of the world.

Just like the weather, the market does not conform to any rules of behavior. And that's something to think long and hard about if you're working with an unskilled financial advisor—or if you've decided to do it yourself.

From your perspective, the market may appear to be moving in one direction, but from a larger perspective, it could moving in many different directions at the same time. When you monitor a storm closely on weather radar, you can observe this majestic natural phenomenon—fronts moving in one direction while the storm itself goes in another. Just like the weather, the market's apparent direction may not be its true one.

Many people conclude that they're experienced investors because they've been up and down in the market a few times. But that just isn't so. Like wind, waves, and currents, investments behave differently in various conditions and circumstances. If you aren't familiar with all of these conditions and haven't experienced and navigated them, then you are not experienced.

> **Many people conclude that they're experienced investors because they've been up and down in the market a few times. But that just isn't so.**

The same is true for your advisor. And that's why the skilled, fee-only advisor concept is so valuable in both calm and turbulent waters.

* * *

By now, you're probably wondering what to do. When all is said and done, what's right for you?

In deep-sea voyages, passages are principal routes between key places. In the Caribbean, the Windward and Mona Passages are famous for their dangerous waters. These passages contain strong tidal flows between the major islands that cause the seas to become unexpectedly violent.

In your voyage to retirement, you can choose a similar passage—a commission-based advisor whose decisions and advice may be driven by corporate-level executives or by the commissions and incentives of the investment companies themselves.

Or you might choose another passage—the do-it-yourself one. You can be the skipper of your own boat, but can you recognize the tidal flows and stay out of troubled waters? Good seamanship can get you out of most situations, but if you find out too late that you just don't have the skills you need, you may capsize your retirement.

Or you can take a third passage—one that offers the best chance for a smooth voyage to a profoundly beautiful retirement.

That's the passage of the skilled, fee-only advisor, one who voluntarily waives commissions and incentives in order to focus on the life management of his clients.

To find out more about who I am and what I do, I hope you'll review all the information and videos I've posted on **www.StormproofRetirement.com.**

Whatever passage you ultimately choose, I hope it's the right one for you. I want your retirement to be everything you've dreamed of.

Bon voyage!

CPSIA information can be obtained
at www.ICGtesting.com
Printed in the USA
JSHW052341260322
24280JS00003B/15